Word of MOUSE - Today's "Word of Mouth" Marketing:

How to Use Social Media in Small Business for Take-it-to-the-BANK Results

"Viver" Winters Israel

Copyright © November 2013 Vivianne "Viver" Winters Israel

All rights reserved.

Dedication

This book is dedicated to small business owners everywhere. You are the backbone of our country and vital to its economic recovery. It is your passion, enthusiasm, creativity, commitment, and sheer tenacity which allow for a constant flow of new ideas, new products, new services, new experiences, and new technologies with an agility which rivals that of larger corporate structures.

Disclaimer

This book is designed to provide information on online social media and mobile marketing only. This information is provided and sold with the knowledge that the publisher and author do not offer any legal or other professional advice. In the case of a need for any such expertise consult with the appropriate professional. This book does not contain all information available on the subject. This book has not been created to be specific to any individual's or organizations' situation or needs. Every effort has been made to make this book as accurate as possible. However, there may be typographical and or content errors. Therefore, this book should serve only as a general guide and not as the ultimate source of subject information. This book contains information that might be dated and is intended only to educate and entertain. The author and publisher shall have no liability or responsibility to any person or entity regarding any loss or damage incurred, or alleged to have incurred, directly or indirectly, by the information contained in this book.

Table of Contents

Acknowledgments iii

Introduction v
    How to Use This Book v

How To Create The "Secret Sauce" Currently Missing From Your Marketing Messages 7
    Status Quo Marketing: Messages With No "Secret Sauce" 8
    So What's Wrong? 8
    Marketing Then vs. Today's Marketing Message Tsunami 9
    What's Missing from the Message is "Business-Critical" 11
    The Solution 11
    What is The "Secret Sauce"? 13
    How Customers/Prospects Search for What They Want 14
    A Daydream Marketing Exercise 16
    Discovering the 'Base' to YOUR "Secret Sauce" Recipe 17
    YOUR "Secret Sauce" Recipe 'Base': Step-by-Step 17
    Who's Doing It Right? 18
    Adding Extras to Your "Secret Sauce"—A Gift That Keeps on Giving 20
    Presenting Your 'Gift' Correctly 22
    What We've Covered, So Far 24
    Once Upon a—Business—Time 25
    Why is 'Story' so Important? 26
    Will the REAL "Target Audience" Please Stand Up? 29
    Is Your Marketing Message "Sticky"? 30
    Worksheet: My Marketing To Do List 34

Why Social Media Can Prove To Be The Most Powerful Tool In Your Marketing Arsenal 35
    What is "Word of Mouth" Marketing . . . Traditionally? 35
    "Word of Mouth" Marketing Gets an Upgrade! 37

"Word of Mouth" Becomes 'Word of MOUSE' 37
Doing Your Part for Good 'Word of MOUSE' 39
Human Nature and Negative 'Word of MOUSE' Marketing 39
A Social Media Marketing Example: Business Goes From Zero to Hero in 24 Hours.. 41
Does Anyone Have Social Media Marketing Figured Out? .. 45
A Mobile Marketing Example: Making a Difference for Business in Record Time.. 46
Make Social Media a Game-Changer for YOUR Business.... 49

Why Retaining Control Of YOUR "Business Voice" In Your Social Media Is A Primary Business Survival Tactic 51
What is "Business Voice"?.. 51
Why Do Business Owners Give Away Their Power . . . The Power of Their "Business Voice"? 52
Who Are You Trusting With Your "Business Voice"?........... 53
One Scenario of Losing Your "Business Voice" 56
Choosing YOUR business to be Your "Business Voice"....... 59
Business IS Personal 62

Where to Find Untapped Treasures Of Content For Your Social Media That Already Exist Within Your Business 65
How Will I Find Time to Create Social Media Content?........ 65
Where to Find YOUR Hidden 'Content Treasures' 66
How to Make the MOST of Each Piece of Content 67
Worksheet: My Possible Sources for Content Treasures...... 70

Where to Start: Making Sense of Social Media & Which Types are Appropriate for YOUR Business 71
Getting Familiar With The Most Effective Types of Social Media for Your Business.. 71
What Exactly is Social Media? 72
Pinterest—More Important for Business Than Most People Realize! 73
What About Google+ ? 76
Should I Use LinkedIN for Marketing? 76
Can Twitter Really be Used as a Serious Marketing Tool? 78

Twitter for Speakers 79
Twitter—Life's Blood for Food Trucks 80
Twitter Brings Crowds to a New Business Within 3 Hours.. 81
Selling Computers via Twitter 82
What About Purely Local Business: Gardeners, Plumbers, Cleaners, Etc.? 84
Customer Review Sites & Online Directories with a Local Search Function 84
Facebook as a Social Media Marketing Channel 85
Why Can't Facebook Be My Business Blog? 86
The Magic of Closed/Private Facebook Groups 87
But I Don't Have Time To Keep Checking My Computer for Posts To My Social Media 89
Can Creating YouTube Videos Make You A How-To Expert? 89
Owning Your Own Marketing Channels Is Vital! 91
Which Channels Should be The Core of Your Social Media Marketing? 92
What IS A Blog? 92
Your Blog: Your Most Powerful Marketing Tool 93
Why Are Blogs So Great For Search Engine Optimization (SEO)? 94
Your Email List And Email Marketing 96
Podcasting—The Under-utilized Gold Mine Of Marketing . 96
But What About My Traditional Marketing, You Ask? 97
How to Give Social Media Marketing a Chance in Your Business, With an Already Fixed Budget 98

How to Almost Painlessly Incorporate A Social Media Marketing Campaign Into Your Regular Business Operations and Not Just as Something Else To Be Done 99

Digging for Your Content Treasures, Step-by-Step 100
More Hidden Content Treasure 102
Your First 'Treasure Council' Meeting Agenda 102
Deciding on a Frequency for Publishing Your Social Media Content 105

Will You Give Up The Power of "Your Business Voice"?. 105
Get Your Own People Involved in "Your Business Voice"! 106
A Plan for the One-Woman/One-Man Business 107
An Exercise for "Finding" The Time You Need for Social Media 108
Do Your Marketing Videos Need to be Fancy & Polished? 110
What If I Don't Have the Right Look for Video? What If I'm Not a Great Speaker? 111
How Long is a "Short Video"? 111
Determining The Right Length for Your Videos 112
What About Podcasting? 112
Which Channels of Social Media Marketing Will You Start With? 113
Reviewing The Process You've Learned 115
What To Do Next Checklist—Step-by-Step 115
If You Get Stuck, Call Me! 117
What Do I Do As A Social Media Marketing Consultant? . 118
Apply for a FREE Consultation 119

About The Author **121**

More Resources from MIYPmarketing.com

Questions about social media?
Go to Word of MOUSE Blog
at WordOfMouseBlog.com
&
Listen to Word of MOUSE Podcast.
New episodes 2nd & 4th Tuesday each month.
Available on iTunes

Want help with your top business challenges?
Listen to some real-world examples from interviews with fellow business owners, who also share their best, and worst, marketing efforts, their biggest business regret and their best business tip on *The Small Businesses Solving BIG Problems Show w/ Viver Israel* New episodes on the 1st & 3rd Tuesday each month.
Available on iTunes

Know someone who is 80+ years old?
Help them share their wisdom and insights with the world—
Go to Treasured Wisdom Archive
at MIYPmarketing.com/Treasured-Wisdom

COMING SOON

Website CPR Solution
Breathe life into non-performing Websites & Social Media by completing this FREE online checklist. Website CPR Solution pinpoints marketing problems in Websites as well as social media marketing usage, then generates real-world solutions you can put into action. *Available December 2013*

Home Study Course
Word of MOUSE – Today's "Word of Mouth" Marketing:
How to Use Social Media in Small Business
for Take-it-to-the BANK Results
Available 1st Quarter 2014

Viver Winters Israel

Acknowledgments

Heartfelt gratitude to my mentors, instrumental in guiding this manuscript to completion: Alicia Dunams' amazing Bestseller in a Weekend program that turbo-boosted the flow of content, Christine Kloser for her mind-opening Transformational Author Conference, Gail Larsen for the incredible treasures found in her book *Transformational Speaking*, and to the generous Fran Harris of Made for TV Academy for her timely suggestions in fine-tuning the cover art.
Many thanks, for your inspiration and coaching!

Introduction

What if . . . the customers / clients who need what you do in your business came flocking to your storefront, or Website?

What difference would that make in your life?

What difference would that make in your finances?

What would your business look like if that happened?

Does this sound like a fantasy, because it's not what you are currently experiencing in your business? The ability to bring that image much closer to a take-it-to-the-**bank** reality can rest in a simple shift of how you develop your marketing messages and where and how those messages are delivered.

This shift will result in:

- many more potential customers discovering that your business exists
- more of those prospects who have newly discovered your business wanting to learn more about what you have to help them
- developing those new potential customers into paying customers
- getting more referrals from both happy customers and happy "followers" of your business' informational content

'Word of MOUSE' is today's "word of mouth" marketing. This electronic re-expression of word of mouth travels at far faster speeds and is available for viewing, reviewing and interpretation at the incredible speed of today's technology.

How to Use This Book

To get the most out of time spent with this book, grab some

note paper and a pen, your digital recording device, your cassette recording device, or simply open the voice recorder app in your smartphone. As you read, thoughts and ideas about your business' marketing will come to you. Make the most of these thoughts and ideas by writing them down or recording them while they are fresh in your mind.

HOT TIP

Go to www.WordOfMouseBlog.com/workbook to download your FREE Word Of MOUSE Companion Workbook!

(Look for more **HOT TIPS** throughout the book)

1

How To Create The "Secret Sauce" Currently Missing From Your Marketing Messages

What is it that's missing from your current advertising strategy? As a fellow business owner, I know you put a great deal of thought and effort into your marketing messages. Whether print advertisement, direct mail piece, a brochure, Website page or part of a social media campaign, you want your marketing message to be the best representation of your business. You want it to tell prospective customers why they should choose your company to satisfy their needs. However, unless your business falls within a certain very small percentage, there is an element missing from your marketing messages.

So, let's get started on the path toward designing **your** "Secret Sauce" recipe! First, I'm going to share a little background information with you about marketing messages, which will lead us to what it is that's missing. Then we'll talk about that seemingly illusive, missing element. Once you have a grasp on what the missing element is, then we can get into the "Secret Sauce."

Status Quo Marketing: Messages With No "Secret Sauce"

There exist tons upon tons of marketing in our world: in print, in display ads, and on the Internet. Almost all of it focuses on the companies which are doing the marketing; meaning, the marketing messages are about how Company X: is #4 in their overall industry, the best of their industry in their home state or county, have this or that award for [fill in the blank], or even have been in business since Christopher Columbus landed in the New World. These ads are also focusing on the products and/or services they offer, including their features and benefits.

You may be thinking, "Well, of course! The business needs to state their standing in their industry. If they are highly recognized, have a long legacy of being in business, or display testimonials from satisfied customers—if they can. That's what inspires confidence in potential customers. So these potential customers choose **that** business over another competing business. That **is** the purpose of marketing."

And, if this is your thought, you would be correct. That is what marketing is and what marketing has been for decades—the development of messages that profess the awesome-ness of a company. It starts with how one business owner's company is better than Company B or Company C because of the features of their product, the length of time they have been in business, the quality of their product, and their dedication to customer service, etc.

So What's Wrong?

In the above example, I painted a very generic illustration of most of the marketing we see and hear, Company X claims its awesome-ness is greater than Company B or Company C, examples of their competition. Let's call that generic example Company A.

Well, just as you know everything about your business, Company A's owner knows everything about Company A. And just like you, Company A's owner is committed to having his/her marketing materials represent his/her Company in the best manner possible. However, Company A is speaking from **its** perspective—the perspective of Company A; how great their products and services, are, how great Company A is, what high percentages they may have achieved in their Quality Assurance, how they are the #1, or #2, or #10 out of 400,000 businesses that provide the same products/services, and why we should buy their stuff instead of buying from Company B or Company C, who offer the same, or similar, products/services.

Yes, that is the third time I've made the point that marketing messages drone on and on about their business. This point is "business-critical" so I want to be certain I've driven the point into your thinking.

Still, what exactly is wrong . . . ? Company A, as well as a minimum of 85+ % of business marketing media, speaks **only** from the perspective of the business **not** from the perspective of the customer they hope to attract to their business.

Marketing Then vs. Today's Marketing Message Tsunami

Has this manner of marketing worked? Yes, it has—notice the past tense. Can it still work? Yes, but it is far less effective than it was in its "hey-day." Consumers now are far more sophisticated. Back in the 1940s, for instance, catalogs, newspapers, flyers, magazines and radio delivered marketing messages were the norm. Some people were actually excited to see advertisements, since ads were the primary way to discover new possibilities in what was available. You just had to say how great your company was, what you had to offer, and how customers could get what you had. If your product/service was something the customer was looking for or wanted to have and could afford—done deal.

While I wasn't around in the 1940s, I have been around since the mid 1950s. No, I'm not going to tell you exactly how old I am; girls don't do that. And the older we get, the less inclined we are to offer such 'classified' information. But why should you care about (approximately) how old I am? Purely due to the great variety of marketing I have experienced and been involved with, in my time. Believe it or not, I actually started working regularly at the ripe old age of three, in a field where I was actually **part** of the marketing—working as a fashion and photography model. So, while I do not have any formal degrees in marketing, I have been involved in the business since well before I started kindergarten. Now that you have my credentials, back to our brief journey through the recent history of marketing.

In the first few decades of television, the volume of marketing messages a given person watched, read, or heard over the course of a day was easily tolerated. According to Jay Walker-Smith of Yankelovich Consumer Research, back in 1970 the average person was exposed to apx. 500 advertisements each day.

Fast-forward to the early 1990s, which was also the infancy of the commercial aspect of the Internet, and the daily exposure had increased to about 5,000 advertising messages per day. A recent study that actually reflects values from 2009, estimated that the average person is exposed to nearly 30,000 marketing messages each day. And mind you, those values are from 2009.

So, where are all of these marketing messages? From the time, you get up in the morning, when you notice the tags on the clothes you will wear that day, the logos on the components of your breakfast or coffee, the banner ads during your TV or online news, and the mass of marketing emails—add to that the logos on cars, trucks and buses, roadside billboards, bench billboards, on the radio, that pen someone gave you, the vendors you pass . . . everywhere you are flooded with marketing messages. And you haven't even gotten to work yet.

Exactly how many of those marketing messages do you remember from yesterday? From this morning? I can almost see the blank expression on your face . . . the answer is, probably, next to none of them. Maybe two or three. Of those you do remember, did any of them leave you with a positive, or favorable impression?

A boat-load, correction, make that a "**planet**-load" of change has taken place since this predominating style of marketing message was "crowned" effective. Yet, with all of the new possibilities for delivering our marketing messages, the messages themselves have barely changed. Sure the graphics are richer, the delivery flashier but the message is eerily familiar, "Hi! We're the best; forget the rest. Buy our stuff!" Multiply that by 30,000 per prospective customer, per day.

Is it really any wonder that yester-years preferred marketing technique has become less effective? Your potential customers; everyone's potential customers have become effectively immune to traditional marketing messages.

What's Missing from the Message is "Business-Critical"

What's missing . . . ? Any focus on what their customers and potential customers need. What problems their potential customer has. Whether he/she is currently in need of any one, or more, of the products or services Company A has to offer. Such messages aren't speaking TO their prospective customer, they are talking AT him or her. Customers aren't interested in reading, or hearing, your company resume. In today's marketplace, that missing element— acknowledgement of the potential customers' needs—is "business-critical" to turning your marketing message into a customer and prospect magnet!

The Solution

What is the Solution . . . ? Shift the focus of your marketing message to serving your customers' needs. From a consumer's point of view, marketing is largely a din of "white noise." They aren't even going to take conscious notice of it unless something about a particular message 'speaks' to them; that is, speaks to a need, suggests a solution to a problem they have, offers the answer to a question, or satisfies a curiosity.

Also, your business needs to be producing more than just one piece of good information for your prospective customers to discover. You need to produce customer-focused information on a regular basis, through articles, blog posts, Frequently Asked Questions, podcasts, and/or short how-to videos. Provide reasons for your prospective customers to come back to you/your business/your Website. If they have reason to go back to you when they have other questions about [something prospect needs], you/your business will be in their thoughts, "Oh, I'll go check Karen's site because I know there's going to be a video there about how to do [something prospect needs] or there's going to be a checklist for [something prospect needs]. Besides, when I 'search' for [something prospect needs], what comes up is usually from Karen. So, I might as well just go to Karen's site, and not have to spend 20 minutes navigating through dozens of websites to find my answer!"

This solution is also the 'base' ingredient for your "Secret Sauce." You must shift your marketing messages from being all about your company to being all about serving the needs of your prospective customer, your target audience.

Are you thinking that this sounds too warm and fuzzy, too wishy-washy, too altruistic to be a change that will translate to money in your pocket? I assure you this is the best and surest way to increase your sales.

Some proof: in today's marketplace, 78% of all shoppers use the Internet to research and make purchase choices, according to the most recent report from Cisco Internet Business Solutions Group (IBSG). This Cisco group addresses the trends and market transitions reshaping the consumer landscape. Two years ago, this same report reflected 57%.

Why does this matter to you? Well, there are several reasons. First, it illustrates why your business needs an online presence—an **effective** online presence. If your business does not have an online presence already, that is definitely an item for your

Marketing To Do List. See the last page of Chapter One to start your Marketing To Do List. Or go to WordOfMouseBlog.com/workbook to download your FREE Word Of MOUSE Companion Workbook!

HOT TIP

Unless you can demonstrate an effective return on investment from any print Yellow Pages ads that you have, it's time to give some serious thought to discontinuing that tactic, before your renewal comes due. Those marketing dollars may prove a great deal more effective, directed to another marketing platform.

Second: shifting your marketing messages to being customer-focused will be the 'base'—the core ingredient—of **your** "Secret Sauce." But that's not all! Yes, I know, that sounds too much like certain TV commercials you may have heard. What can I say, I couldn't help myself. ☺ Seriously though, more can be added to your "Secret Sauce." Adding some "extra flavorings," so to speak, to your "Secret Sauce" will make your new marketing messages even more powerful; providing the foundation toward also making your marketing memorable. Memorable marketing is a core element to an even greater volume of referrals as well as inspiring more repeat business. Assuming, of course, you want lots of referrals and more repeat business.

What is The "Secret Sauce"?

The "Secret Sauce" is a weaving together of your prospective customer's needs, 'story', and "stickiness" such that your marketing message, attracts, resonates and 'sticks' with the prospective customer who reads it. Mind you, the "Secret Sauce" is not a one-size fits all. Don't despair, this a good thing, a very good thing. If the "Secret Sauce" were a one-size fits all solution, it would quickly become over-used and rapidly de-evolve into a non-solution for those using it.

No, the "Secret Sauce" will be specific to your business. It will be YOUR "Secret Sauce"!

Allow me to explain. When we talked about the element missing from most marketing messages, we arrived at the solution. A very simple solution. Yet, the fact that something is simple does not mean that it will be easy. In fact, re-crafting your marketing messages with this shift may prove quite a challenge. I also mentioned that if the "Secret Sauce" was a one-size fits all solution, it would quickly become over-used and rapidly de-evolve into a non-solution for those using it; yes, I'm repeating myself—because this point is **very** important!

Keep in mind, **you** have **the most** to gain by making that shift. You are gaining more traffic/visitors to your storefront and/or Website and more paying customers from those visitors. This is a gain that can continue to grow **because** your "Secret Sauce" **isn't** a one-size-fits-all. What business owner doesn't want that sort of growth?!

How Customers/Prospects Search for What They Want

You now have proof that most prospective customers search online for what they are looking to buy. So, when **your** prospective customers search online, do you believe that they search for "which company sells the most widgets in [fill in area where you live]" or "which company selling widgets has been in business since Columbus landed in the New World" or "which company that sells widgets is number five, or better, in their industry"? The correct answer is, No.

Are they searching for "widgets [fill in your area]" or widgets [fill in your city/county/region]"? The answer is, Yes.

Most importantly, are they searching by asking a specific question about a problem they have, such as: "How do I stop a toilet from leaking?" or "What happens during an acupuncture treatment?" or "Which questions should I ask when choosing a Website designer?" The answer is, Yes!

These searches are a large part of the reason why shifting your marketing message to focus on the needs of your prospective customer can turn into money in your pocket.

Let's say that one of your prospective customers has started a search online for a new gas BBQ grill. He is a family man with children, with the youngest at age four. Before buying, before even choosing the model he wants, this Dad wants to know if there is anything in particular he should look for or avoid, when choosing his BBQ grill, considering he has a young child in his household. Dad's search returns over 25 web pages for him to review.

In this example, **you** are in the business of selling BBQ grills and outdoor furnishings, yet your Website did not show up in Dad's search results. As it turns out, most of the other search results didn't really have the information Dad was looking for. Three of the results revealed some information but that information was written from the company's perspective and not really what Dad needed. Then there was one result that had the information Dad needed and was written from Dad's perspective, addressing his concern for the safety of his youngest child once there was a BBQ grill on the back patio. Dad appreciated finding exactly the information he needed. Dad noticed that this Website belonged to a business which also has a physical storefront across town. After going through the information he needed and checking out several BBQ grill models, Dad got in the car and drove to the store across town that had provided the information he needed.

Now, this is a nice example, but there is something wrong with it. What's wrong is: your BBQ and backyard furnishings store has a larger variety of BBQ grills than the one across town. Your business is also a lot closer to where Dad lives. Does Dad know about your store? Whether he knew about your store or not, it was the store across town that had the solution to Dad's problem. He went there because he felt that business understood his problem and would be able to help him make a truly safe choice of BBQ grill for his family.

Your prospective customers are going to be drawn to the information that sounds like it's working to solve their problem as well as to the source which provided that information. **That** customer-focused search result should have been on **your** Website, from **your** business!

A Daydream Marketing Exercise

Imagine prospective customers searching for answers to their questions or solutions to their problems—questions or problems that have to do with the products/services your business offers. Then imagine, that among the best results from their search are a blog post, an article, a how-to video, or Frequently Asked Question (FAQ) which was posted on **your** website. And when they reach for that answer, it is you, your business, providing the answer to their question. What is that worth to you?

Now, being in the business that you are in, you probably know several things about your target audience—those individuals who need your products or services. Such as, what types of problems would someone who needs your products/services have? What challenges might they face?

If you can list some of the problems and challenges that your ideal customers have and create a variety of materials (special reports, blog posts, videos, podcasts, etc.) which solve each of those problems, answers those questions, or satisfy those curiosities, you can position your business as the one prospects turn to for answers. You can position your business as the business which solves their problems. And if, when your prospective customers are searching for solutions, the best and better results that come up are from your business, **you** become the solution to their problem. How powerful is **that**?

When your prospective customer is searching for information details about a product/service, they might also ask "How is a certain product made," "How is service X structured," or "What goes on behind the scenes of a business that makes your products or provides your services? When their best search results come from your business, you are again positioning your business as a source of solutions for them.

As prospective customers see, and continue to see, your business being the source which answers their questions, provides solutions to their problems, and satisfies their curiosity, those prospects also start to identify you as an expert in your field. It is then that a trust relationship begins forming with those prospective customers.

When those prospects need to purchase the products/services you provide, which business storefront or Website are they are more likely to go to for that purchase? The storefront / Website / business owner that they have come to know as an expert and have grown to trust, of course! Wouldn't you want that business, that business owner, to be **YOU**?

Discovering the 'Base' to YOUR "Secret Sauce" Recipe

When the content of your marketing messages is customer-focused (focused on the needs and problems of your target audience with information and keywords important to these prospects), your business is **far more likely to be found during online searches**. It is also more likely to be remembered, whether it was seen online or offline, because you are speaking **to** your prospective customer rather than pushing your business **at** them. No one likes to be **"sold,"** but most everyone likes to **buy** things they want.

YOUR "Secret Sauce" Recipe 'Base': Step-by-Step

1. Write all your marketing messages content from the perspective of your target audience—online and offline. Talk **to** your prospects, not **at** them.
2. Carefully review all marketing messages to make certain they contain words and phrases that your target audience would use when searching for what **they** want. *Caution*: be certain you are talking **to your prospects** rather than search engines. Avoid becoming obsessed and over-packing your messages with keyword after keyword, such that your messages no longer sound like people talking to each other. Search

engines are targeting-"tools," not your target audience.
3. Be the solution to the problems your target audience is likely to have, by providing relevant content on your Website
4. Be the source of answers to the questions your target audience is likely to have, by providing relevant content on your Website.
5. Be the source of answers to the curiosities your target audience is likely to have, by providing relevant content on your Website.
6. Decide upon a plan for how often you will add new content to your Website—remember these are **new** reasons for prospects to visit your marketing messages, and new opportunities to strengthen your 'expert' position as well as develop the trust of your target audience.

And all of this is **without** paying for AdWords and expensive SEO (Search Engine Optimization) strategies! When your marketing messages and Website content are focused on serving your customers, including thoughtful consideration of which keywords your customers and target audience would most likely be using, your Website content IS your SEO strategy.

HOT TIP

Be your own SEO (Search Engine Optimization) strategist: 1) Develop marketing messages that focus on serving the needs of your customer and potential customers (your target audience); 2) create additional informational content that solves the problems your target audience is likely to have, answers the questions they are likely to have, and satisfies the curiosities they may have about how you do what you do in your business; 3) then review those content pieces with thoughtful consideration, making certain the keywords your target audience will most likely be using are within each of your content pieces.

Who's Doing It Right?

While representing only a very small percentage of the businesses involved in marketing both online and offline, there are businesses are out there that do already create their marketing messages from the perspective of their target audience. Would it surprise you to discover that those businesses which develop their messages in this manner are also particularly successful? A few examples: at the Enterprise level include Coca Cola, Proctor & Gamble, and Red Bull; on the small business level, there are "River Pools & Spas" in the U.S. state of Virginia and Dinesen Flooring in Denmark.

I know what you're thinking. Well, yeah! Coca Cola, Proctor & Gamble (P&G), Red Bull—they have MASSIVE UBER-budgets. They can pursue any marketing idea they want. What can that possibly have to do with my **small** business? Yes, Enterprise-level businesses have budgets which, if we say them out-loud, could make us break out in a zero-envy rash. We can't play in their 'financial' ballpark. However, we can emulate their strategies by acting on what these businesses, collectively, are doing right. We can also realize not all Enterprise-level businesses are doing it right; actually, most of them are not. So, money is not **the** difference. Insight, choice and execution, through resourceful and creative emulation, **is** the difference. And small business owners **can** capitalize on that difference.

The Enterprise business examples above are not each utilizing **all** of the powerful pieces of effective customer-focused marketing. Only Red Bull is doing it all! I've spent a few years reviewing and studying thousands of Websites and several hundred businesses, looking for what works and what doesn't in marketing, particularly since the advent of social media. I now get a kick out of imagining where these already 'big boy companies' would be, financially, if they each did use all of the customer-focused 'power tools'!

But what I actually get excited about is what creative, resourceful emulation of these strategies can do for small business owners. That is why I am on a mission to revolutionize how small business owners develop their marketing messages; because doing so is a **serious** game-changer at the level of small business. It can be the difference between closing down your business and keeping it alive, or even moving it to a strengthened source of revenue. It can be the difference between feeling as though you "own a job" versus actually running a business, the difference between being enslaved by your business and your business benefiting you and your customers!

HOT TIP

We've talked a LOT about "your target audience." If you are not certain which individuals make up your target audience OR you believe that your target audience is everyone then setting aside some time to focus on identifying who your target audience is—by developing a profile of your two most ideal customers—is an item for your Marketing To Do List! There is an online tool to help with this. This tool was designed for companies involved in business-to-business transactions. However, going through this process may help spur ideas for those of you that are business-to-consumer businesses: http://upcloseandpersona.com.

Adding Extras to Your "Secret Sauce"—A Gift That Keeps on Giving

Okay, you know you've heard this from your family, friends, acquaintances, strangers—a good 1000+ times, if you've heard it once: references to 'gifts that keep on giving.' Quite probably, this was for both positive *and* negative examples. This discussion focuses on positive results. In this instance, I am not talking about free reports as an enticement for a prospect to provide their email address, etc. I'm not even talking about a "value added" bonus which you might include with a product, service or information product.

Here, I am talking about another opportunity to be of service to your target audience; providing a gift to them. A gift that will indeed, keep on giving, to **you** as well as to your target audience. This "Secret Sauce" additive requires ongoing attention. However, this additive can also be a core component to "brand building" and acting as a catalyst toward growing rewards through your new marketing strategy. That is, rewards for your target audience **and** your business' bottom line.

What is the gift? The gift is your business providing some source of digital information—a blog, podcast, Facebook Group, an "Ask Annie / Ask Us" Website or a separate area of your exiting Website—which addresses one or two challenges or concerns shared by individuals in your target audience. And you provide these resources . . . **without any selling**!

This is a bit of a trust, leap-of-faith piece. But if you provide an information venue that addresses issues especially relevant to your target audience that aren't part of your actual, going-out-there marketing, it will make a big difference to your target audience.

It isn't that you can't have, somewhere in your graphic or at the byline: this blog/venue is authored or managed by MyCompany.com. But it cannot have anything that really tries to take them back to your products/services or says, "Oh, hey, click here to see our great products/services." There can be nothing that tries to bring their visit to a sale.

This is just your business providing information that is valuable to your target audience. You are building relationships, which lead to trust. And when prospects trust you, they're going to end up coming to you when they do need a product or a service that you offer. They will automatically come to you instead of searching for someone else.

This will result in sales. It just doesn't do so initially. This strategy is slightly indirect but still amazingly powerful. It has already made amazing differences for large businesses and even small businesses, such as River Pools & Spas in the state of Virginia. This approach is worthy. Yes, it's different, but it's worth your time and effort!

The information can be in a domain you own, even a section of your main domain. But you must do your 'marketing' of your "gift area" to point your target audience to exactly where that information exists! Do not say, "Go to OurMainWebsite.com and click on such-and-such particular link" to direct prospects to access your "gift information" area. What you **do** say is "Go to OurWebsite.com/specialized_information" or "Go to SpecializedInformation.com." It is okay, as well as important, to have subtle branding somewhere on the Web pages of your 'gift' area whether that area is within your primary domain or on a separate domain, which you may decide to set up for this information.

Presenting Your 'Gift' Correctly

Keep in mind, I did say **subtle** branding. Displaying "MyMASSIVEbusinesslogo" on every page is not subtle branding. You **do** want those who come across this "specialized information" to *be able to know* that it is your business providing the information. However, you **do not** want to beat your Website visitors over the head with this fact OR sell your wares and/or services in this specialized area. Utilizing what is supposed to be a gift area for your target audience, to sell, advertise, or dazzle your Web visitors with massive logos or branding would not provide the desired results. It would end up being only a less functional expression of your main Website and become a colossal waste of your time and energy.

"Show me an example of a 'gift' for a target audience," you say. Okay! Using Proctor and Gamble (P&G) as an example, their variety of products includes feminine hygiene products. You can relax, you will survive hearing this seemingly intimate example. It simply is the best single example to illustrate my point. Come on, we're all adults here.

Take a deep breath. Okay, one more time . . . The enormous variety of products that P&G offers, includes feminine hygiene products. One of the non-selling 'gifts' that P&G decided to offer was a Website to specifically be of assistance to young girls who are about to or have just recently 'entered puberty.' The site is a hub for information, an archive of questions/answers and an online community with an "Ask Me" feature. It's formatted to be like girlfriends talking to each other. Everything at this site is meant to help young girls by addressing questions, concerns, fears, and myths about the changes they are, or are about to, experience in their lives.

This is a place they can visit, privately, to ask questions they might yet be too embarrassed to ask their parents. At this site, they can get more reliable information than that of well-meaning, though misinformed, friends. This single site, BeingGirl.com, has helped hundreds of thousands of young girls. Did I forget to mention there is also a site for Moms and Dads in search of help on how to approach and manage discussing the topic with their growing daughter(s)?!

None of these pieces link back directly to Proctor and Gamble. This is just information for these girls and a separate site for the parents. There is branding, to a point, as far as color scheme and logo, but the information there is truly just to help some of P&G's target audience find information they need.

Yes, P&G is already a giant business. But what if your business had come up with that 'gift' idea? What difference might that have made for the growth and financial standing of your business? So, put on your thinking cap . . . What could you come up with for your business to provide as a gift to your target audience? Your 'gift' to your target audience does not need to be huge or expensive. It only needs to be on-target for your target audience. And who knows, some time in the relatively near future, you might end up coming up with another 'gift' idea, a super-power solution for your target audience. One that ends up making an even greater difference to the bottom line of your business.

HOT TIP

Don't try to work in all the extra flavorings for your business' "Secret Sauce" before you start working on developing your new marketing messages. Get your basic "Secret Sauce" working for you. The very process of re-crafting your marketing messages, the work you do to decide on what those messages will be, will prove valuable information for when you do start working on adding to your "Secret Sauce." The work you do on creating the base ingredient to your "Secret Sauce" will lay the foundation for your added flavorings. It will also prove more cost-effective to go through your marketing message revolution in stages. Another item for your Marketing To Do List!. Set a future date for this one. Yes, you might need to adjust your date but SET a date. "Someday," does not exist on anyone's calendar; "someday" is not a real point in time. Make this real! Assign an actual date to this item on your Marketing To Do List!

What We've Covered, So Far

Time to rewind and review what we've covered, before exploring the next extra flavoring that could be added to your "Secret Sauce." We know that well over 80% of businesses creating marketing messages are not creating those messages from the perspective of service to their target audience. We know that re-developing your marketing messages from the perspective of your target audience—what they need, what they are looking for—turns you into your own Search Engine Optimization (SEO) Strategist. Your marketing content will be among the best 'search engine candy' there is **and** it will prove far more cost-effective than AdWords or expensive SEO strategies.

We know that the first "extra flavoring" that you can add to your "Secret Sauce" is to create one or two "gifts" for your target audience. Creating "some manner of information venue"—a blog, podcast, Facebook Group, an "Ask Annie / Ask Us" Website or separate area of your exiting Website—is the gift. This 'gift' addresses one or two challenges or concerns shared by individuals in your target audience. This 'gift' also provides another opportunity for your business to be the solution to the problems of your target audience, to be the source of answers to their questions, and to satisfy their curiosities.

We know that the "gift" changes how a prospect or customer becomes attached to the particular brand or company providing the 'gift.' We know that if you take on developing a 'gift' for your target audience, it will provide even more of a foundation for your target audience to start seeing you as a leader and expert in your field. Further, they start seeing you as someone they can trust, someone they want to do business with.

We know that your "gift" provides another way for your business to develop relationships with your target audience. Not everyone will take on making a 'gift' as part of their "Secret Sauce." It is a big commitment. But it is a commitment that yields excellent pay offs! It attracts more prospects to your storefront/Website and is a catalyst for converting more leads and prospects to paying customers. And that is what you want, isn't it?

Once Upon a—Business—Time

No, this isn't another daydream marketing exercise. It is actually the next level for "upgrading" your "Secret Sauce." This is about taking what you have learned so far, your base recipe for your "Secret Sauce," and adding another game-changing ingredient . . . adding "story"!

What does "story" have to do with business . . .? Everything! Writing your marketing content as a story, speaking to your target audience through story, helps your customer/prospect identify with what's being said in your marketing message. That translates into "your company has what they need." Now, try to tell me that doesn't just make your 'business owner senses' tingle all over! Not only do customers feel you know what their problems are, but through story, you show that you really **understand** them. It improves how your prospect "bonds" with you. Additionally, story multiplies the possibility that your prospect will remember your marketing message!

We've talked about how today's consumer is practically "immune" to the nearly 30,000 marketing messages they are bombarded with every day. We know now that customers aren't really interested in hearing your business resume, proclaiming how great your business is. They want to hear that someone cares about them and what they need. They want to hear from someone who has 'walked a mile in their shoes; or just know that they are listening to someone who knows what it is that they (the target audience) want. If you want your message to do more than get through that 'white noise' of 30,000 per day marketing messages, if you want your message to really resonate, or 'ring true,' for your target audience, then 'story' is the tool to use. Story can ensure your message stands apart from the 'marketing din' that your target audience is exposed to on a daily basis.

As humans, we want stories. Humans LOVE stories. Granted, most of us don't move through our day, thinking, "Wow, I haven't heard a story today. I really need to hear a good story." Still, I believe it is easy enough to demonstrate that humans crave 'story.' Don't you enjoy reading books—novels, biographies, autobiographies, science fiction? Whatever kind of reading you prefer, there is an element of story.

Do you enjoy magazines or newspapers—online or offline? Lots of story there. The same with movies. And while you may not watch television, how much time do most of the people you know spend watching television? Television is **full** of story. Movies, dramas, comedies, talk shows, even sports commentaries and news shows—all **full** of story.

Why is 'Story' so Important?

Let's say you are re-crafting your marketing messages. You have written a new article/blog post and published it to the blog on your business Website. This new article has been on your site for a couple of weeks now and you're a little excited about it because it is already attracting more readers than any of your previous posts. So, something new is happening on your Website—more visitors. Maybe some of these visitors are looking through your blog, or even your Website, to see if there's anything else there that will help them.

So, more people are finding the information which you have re-crafted to 'speak' from the perspective of your target audience. Score one for you! But getting "eyeballs" to come and see your Website isn't all that is needed. Now that more people are finding your Website information, how long will they stay once they arrive? If they haven't found what they're looking for in 6-8 seconds, they will move on to the next search result! Yes, statistically speaking, that's all you get—6-8seconds of "eyeball time" before a Website visitor moves on to the next result, if they haven't found what they were looking for in your Website. The new article you wrote had to have sounded like information they needed for them to go to your Website. Will that article deliver on the 'promise' it implied? What happens next? Will they:

- start to read and find that it falls short of their expectations, moving on to another search result before they even finish your information?
- read the entire piece but then move on because it

doesn't really answer their question, solve their problem or direct them to the solution to their problem (which may be somewhere else on your Website)?
- read the entire piece, maybe look at something else on your Website and then move on to do some "comparison shopping" before deciding which business/source to choose?
- read your information piece and stop in their tracks, thinking—this is IT. This is exactly what I was looking for, exactly what I need. Then purchase your product from your Website or engage in a live chat to clarify some specification; maybe even hop into their Vespa and motor downtown to your storefront to purchase the item or service in question?

In this instance, suppose the person reads the entire piece, found some specification details elsewhere on your Website, then moved on to do some "comparison shopping" before making their decision. You might be thinking that such a scenario is still a "win!" After all, they found you, they visited your Website. They see that your information is speaking from their perspective. However, they left your site and continued to shop. Now say their comparison shopping resulted in their wanting to come back to your site to make their purchase. They have browsed about 34 sites, 19 of which were possibilities and 8 of which were good candidates. Even though they've determined they **want** to go back to your Website, they may no longer remember which one was yours. They are suffering from 'search overwhelm'.

If only there had been something else included in your article. Something, in addition to your information, which showed that prospective customer that you have what they need. If only there had been something about that information which made it stand out strongly enough that it resonated with their thinking and 'took seed' in their memory, allowing them to remember which Website was yours. If your article had also included a story element, that 'sticky' factor could have triggered their memory of your Website.

If your information not only speaks from the perspective of your target audience but also includes 'story' that information's, source is easier to remember. This is because, unlike most of what they will have seen and read—even the good, on-target information—the information with 'story' will **mean something** to them. It's one thing to provide information that makes sense. It is another thing to produce the information customers are looking for.   It is yet another thing, and at a higher level, to create something that will resonate and have meaning for your potential customers—your target audience.

If your information isn't developed as a story they're going to remember, then: twenty minutes, ten minutes, five minutes later as they continue their Internet search, the information they read on your Website will already be forgotten, like vapor in the wind.

We attach to stories. We identify with stories. Stories speak to us differently than just statistics and information devoid of any 'dressing.'   To be powerful, information should connect to an individual.

If you phrase your marketing message such that you're actually speaking **to** an individual, that individual is going to **hear** your message **quite** differently than, again, just information. Even if it's the information they're looking for. You don't only want to satisfy them with the information they want; you want the message and the information to be remembered! 'Story' adds some "sticky" value to your marketing message.

If a message has some "sticky" value to it, an individual is more likely to remember the message as well as its source. A good story written TO your target audience will resonate with them.   That resonance is a factor of "sticky-ness." A story that resonates in their memory will cause them to remember **you**! That you are where that 'great information piece' came from. Instead of the response . . . "Where did I find that information? . . . No idea. Okay, now I have to start over.   I have to go look for this information again. I'll try searching again. Maybe that piece will show up again in my new search." Do you really want to leave to chance whether that prospect can, again, find your Website?

Having 'story' in your marketing messages magnifies the

recognition of your business in your target audience. Having 'story' woven into your messages can also shorten the timeline for a prospective customer to develop a relationship with you/your business and so, has the potential to move them towards trusting you sooner.

Will the REAL "Target Audience" Please Stand Up?

You will not be able to create effective story in your marketing messages if you see your target audience as being 'everybody.' Perhaps the product/service you have is one that everybody could benefit from. However, there will never be enough people who learn about your amazing product, or service, if you try to market it to everyone on the planet. There is simply no possible way to speak from the perspective of everyone—unless, of course, we are being invaded by flesh-eating bug aliens and you sell some kind of energy pistol that kills those flesh-eating bug aliens.

THEN, yes, everyone will be more than interested. However, in such an instance, supply and demand would have you out of inventory before you know it. Your phenomenal, rapid rise to being an expert, leader, trusted, and even 'desired' individual would quickly pass, as life on this planet ceased to exist. Flesh-eating Alien Bugs – 600 gazillion-million; Humans – Zero. No one/no thing left would need your energy gun, or this book, for that matter. So, there you go, one example where marketing to everybody worked . . . briefly!

Since I am fully confident that my little trip down Sci-fi Lane is not the marketing example you, or any other business owner, is looking for, I will return us to reality and re-state. Short of impending and immediate planetary annihilation, you cannot develop an effective marketing message from the perspective of all-humanity, aka everyone. There is precious little that resonates with everyone.

To effectively develop a marketing message that speaks to "someone," you need a "someone" to speak to. You always need *someone* to tell your story to, which is why it is said, "Don't try to market to everyone because you're then marketing to on one." So, market to *someone*, that *someone* is your target audience. For the best practice, make up a fictitious person who has the likes, dislikes, lifestyle, activities, and probable problems of *someone* that would be in your target audience. This fictitious *someone* is a representation of the individuals which make up your target audience; now create a profile—an "identity"—for this *someone*.

You probably actually have two, maybe three, '*someones*' who represent your ideal customer(s). Create a detailed profile for each of those two, or three, *someones* who would have the highest likelihood of needing/wanting your products/services. With a clearer understanding of who your target audience is, you can truly write marketing messages from the perspective of that *someone*. Give that *someone* a name, a complete identity and you are now even better equipped to add story to your messages; because now you are actually writing to an individual! And **if** that customer profile actually reminds you of a customer you know, or someone you from your personal life, all the better!

BE that person/BE that company, which speaks to your target audience from their perspective, AND add the element of 'story' to compound the impact of your message.

Is Your Marketing Message "Sticky"?

We have touched on "sticky" while we talked about story. However, true "sticky" is more than just story. What is truly "sticky"? A couple of examples will answer most of that question:

- "Where's the beef?"
- "Just do it."
- "The happiest place on earth"
- "Things go better with ___"

"Sticky" is things that **stick** in your mind. For instance, you can probably fill in the blank for the last one, since the above are among the most popular "sticky" phrases. Phrase 'branding' is another term that could replace the word "sticky.' Of course, there is a psychology to stickiness which helps us determine what will resonate with different people.

Let's make up an example. As a business owner, I say, "Okay, here's my marketing message. Now that I have my message, I need to rethink this message. Is this message really speaking from our target audience's point of view?" Well, let's say I have created a customer profile, a fictitious *someone* named "Joe," and the marketing message I've been working on is for Joe's profile. "Joe" is 35 years old and he's had a small business for three years; now he's looking for an answer to a question, and I know I have the service or product that can help him. Is this message something that would matter to him?

If that message wouldn't matter to Joe, then re-write it. Just for laughs, pretend that this hypothetical message means something to a different profile. We'll call this profile "George." George is 85 years old and hasn't gotten out of bed for three weeks; he hasn't purchased anything in five years. George is **not** my target audience. I don't want messages which speak to George. I want to make sure my marketing message speaks to Joe, the young businessman. And I need to make certain that my message focuses on one particular problem he has, so when Joe searches for an answer, for a solution to that problem, he is most likely to find my message in his search results.

I also need to make certain that my marketing message, my answer, for "Joe" is phrased in information and verbiage that makes sense to **him**. The message must come from a story that speaks to Joe's emotion. When I review the message again, I'll be looking for "stickiness." It seems like a lot, I know, but it requires time and effort to go from traditional business-focused messages to customer-focused messages.

It requires even more effort to go from the customer-focused messages to a message which incorporates "story," and further effort to come up with something "sticky." When you are in the early stages of re-developing your marketing messages, your business probably doesn't have time to "reach for the sticky level." However, the additional time and effort is entirely worth it for your flagship product and/or service and any key programs you offer.

As you develop your skills at re-crafting your messages, it will become easier and easier for you to write from the perspective of your target audience. The same can be said of developing your story-writing skills. Over time, writing many messages, answering many questions, solving many problems for your customers—you will begin to identify factors that can help you bring messages to the level of achieving "story."

Achieving the sticky factor for a product, service, or program is the UBER-level of memorable marketing. The "sticky" factor elevates a prospects ability and likelihood to remember your message, your product, over someone else's. Getting to the "sticky" is very hard but getting to the story is vital. As I've mentioned, people don't want to be sold, but everybody loves to buy something they need or something they really want— "Something they can't do without." Always remember: they want to buy, but they don't want to be sold.

It needs to be the small business owner's job, as marketer for his/her own business, to create marketing messages that speak to their customer's needs. You want to be the source of solutions to your customer's problems, the answer to their questions. In today's marketplace, each business actually needs to also be a publisher of information that is a go-to resource for their target audience. This is what is required to stand apart from the marketing messages that everyone is bombarded with on a daily basis.

"Word of MOUSE"—Today's "Word of Mouth" Marketing

Worksheet: My Marketing To Do List

2

Why Social Media Can Prove To Be The Most Powerful Tool In Your Marketing Arsenal

What is "Word of Mouth" Marketing . . . Traditionally?

Word of mouth marketing has always been a best friend of business owners. Your business takes care of a new customer, we'll call him Brandon. Brandon is especially happy with your product/service and shares his positive experience with his wife, his parents, and his brother. A few weeks later, he also talks to someone he overhears at the hardware store, needing the same product/service.

Brandon's hardware store acquaintance comes to you, asking that you take care of him as you took care of Brandon. Later, another new customer comes in. When you ask how they heard about you, they admit hearing about your work from their wife, whose friend's husband talked about how happy he was with the product/service your business provided.

You did not market to these two new customers. One of your very satisfied customers, Brandon, did that marketing for you. These new customers came to you, ready to do business with you, as a result of the quality of business you provided to Brandon. That is an example of word of mouth marketing. If you provide excellent service to these two new customers, they may also 'sing your praises' to people they know, which is how word of mouth marketing continues to grow and positively impact your business.

Word of mouth marketing has been around for millennia. No doubt, even before the use of "money" as we know it, when 'currency' was just the trading of goods or services, there was word of mouth marketing. For example, a farmer might have used a small portion of their crop harvest to trade for a new basket and another water jug. Let's say the farmer preferred Elijah's baskets and jugs, in-trade, instead of Jonah's. Because Elijah's baskets and jugs were stronger and lasted much longer than Jonah's, the farmer recommended Elijah's trade to his friends and family. The way that word of mouth was shared hasn't changed—one person sharing a positive, or negative, 'market' experience with other people.

What has changed is the method a person might utilize to carry that word of mouth message to another individual(s). At one time, they went by foot, walking up to a person and sharing their experience in a conversation. Later they may have ridden an ox-drawn cart to a location and then shared their experience. At some point, maybe they even shared by courier or carrying pigeon.

As we have developed new technologies for travel and communication, the method and speed of sharing our experiences has also changed. We are moving differently, and faster, alongside those evolving travel and communication methods.

Back in the 1930s and 40s, word of mouth marketing was still pretty much person-to-person and by mail. During the 1950s, telephones became common in households. So entered another method of regular person-to-person communication, as well as another vehicle for word of mouth marketing to occur.

"Word of Mouth" Marketing Gets an Upgrade!

The next turbo-boost to communication was e-mail. Technically, e-mail has been around since the 1950s. It was the U.S. Department of Defense's need for an electronic mail network that spawned the ARAPANET, which was the precursor to what we know as the Internet. Email became easier to use and more prevalent over the years. However, the 'faster than a speeding bullet,' nearly instantaneous, and easy to use email that we are familiar with today, has only been widely used, publically, since personal computers became affordable in the early 1990s.

With email people could 'talk' with each other, share stories, favorite movies, as well as whether or not they are happy with a particular purchase of a product or service **instantaneously**! This was a big step for marketing **and** consumers!

Yes, we have all been frustrated by people and businesses who flood our email with SPAM. SPAM is not good—but that is not what I'm talking about here. Right now, I am talking about the progression of communication between people and the increasing speed at which people can share their thoughts and opinions—on the consumer side— through word of mouth marketing.

"Word of Mouth" Becomes 'Word of MOUSE'

As the Internet grew, written, especially conversational, content on the Internet became less predominantly that of educational institutions, governments or businesses producing content directed at individuals and consumers. Somewhere along the way, social networking sites, online customer review sites and other methods by which many people—particularly consumers—are able to communicate with many other peoples in online environments started popping up. The one-to-many and many-to-many models of communication are the essence of the power of social media/social networking.

New technologies developed and new ideas for online social communications were launched or added to existing online venues. These online environments/venues/platforms where many people were sharing their thoughts and opinions with many other people came to be referred to as social networking and finally "social media." There are many opinions as to what first constituted social media. When it started depends on who you listen to, but let's not debate about the timing. What is important is that it started, it grew, it evolved, it became predominant. What matters to you as a business owner is that online social media is a predominating force on the Internet. It has also become a predominating force in commercial business, education, community development, even government, and other organizations.

Word of mouth marketing has gone electronic. Word of mouth is no longer only a one-to-one or one-to-few sharing of a positive or negative experience with a merchant. Word of mouth marketing is now predominantly a one-to-many and many-to-many sharing via social media/social networking. Word of mouth marketing is now email; it's online customer review sites. It's consumers responding to articles/posts on blogs saying what they like and do not like about items, products, services, and businesses. It's consumers publishing their opinions on your business blog, if you have one. If you don't allow comments on your business blog, consumers will post their thoughts on Facebook, Twitter, LinkedIN, Yelp, via a text message to friends, and/or on a consumer blog. Word of mouth has become "Word of MOUSE" . . . communication to many via one, or more, electronic mediums!

Are you thinking, "Sure, that's fine for businesses with a young adult demographic or young family demographics. But the larger part of my target audience is mature adults, 50+ years old." Well, did you know there was a greater than 100% increase in Facebook users aged 55-64 and nearly 150% increase in Twitter users for that same age group over the last twelve months? What are your thoughts now?

Doing Your Part for Good 'Word of MOUSE'

Granted, you have to serve your customers well, for positive word of mouth and word of MOUSE to happen, to continue, and to spread. Prove your integrity to your customers with the information you provide to them and your target audience. Don't ever try to scam your target audience. Any bad content you create will be out there forever unless you pull it down. Keep in mind, there are domains where you can't make the choice to take something "down" once it has been published.

How embarrassing would it be for your business to be stuck with something especially self-serving and over pumped with "fluff" that doesn't help anybody, just to try and make your business look good? Would you want to have shabby Web pages and/or articles still out there and possibly showing up in Internet searches? For the best and long-term results, use this most powerful marketing tool with integrity.

Human Nature and Negative 'Word of MOUSE' Marketing

Social media ushered a quantum leap change in the manner and speed at which people can share their opinions. And that speed is mind-boggling! But remember, word of mouth marketing can be positive or negative. You cannot control word of mouth marketing, you can only influence it. People can, and will, 'sing your praises' in social media when they are delighted with your products, services, and treatment of them during their purchase. However, one unfortunate feature of our human nature is that we tend to share our negative experiences more readily than our positive experiences.

If you're wondering, "Why is she talking about negative word of mouth marketing? Isn't this chapter supposed to be about social media being the most powerful marketing tool?" Yes, this chapter is about social media being the most powerful tool in your marketing arsenal, but negative word of mouth marketing is a fact of life. Remember, human nature includes being more likely to actively share a negative experience than a positive one. A quick recap of that little history of how word of mouth marketing is carried, with a focus on how customers/consumers express complaints, will illustrate how social media is also the most powerful tool in an unhappy customer's arsenal. This social media sword has two edges! This virtual pen has two points! You need to be aware of **both**.

If the word of mouth marketing is negative, gone are the days when a particularly unhappy customer would simply send a letter to your business stating their dissatisfaction with your product/service or their treatment. Consider, how long did that process take? Maybe a little over two weeks, allowing for composing the letter, mailing the letter to your business, then your business responding to that customer. Go-ing are the days when the unhappy customer calls you on the phone to complain, though. The phone call is a fairly quick process unless the customer has difficulty getting through to the person he/she needs to speak with to voice their complaint.

Today, customers who are particularly unhappy with a business's product, service, or treatment of their transaction can send you a scathing email and/or share their upset, **globally**, in a matter of seconds—via Facebook, Yelp, another online customer review site, YouTube, Twitter, and/or blog posts. The point is— social media is an **incredibly** powerful medium for both businesses **and consumers**!

As a business owner, this may leave you feeling especially exposed right now. Are you thinking, "Whoa! That's scary. I'll just keep my business away from this social media stuff so I don't invite 'complainers' and their issues to show up in any social media we might have considered utilizing."

Keeping your business from having its own social media presence does not keep social media from affecting your business. Social media **is** having a powerful effect on your business whether you embrace its use it or not. Either way, the effect it has will only become greater over time. Again, social media will continue to affect your business whether or not your business engages with it.

Remember, you cannot control word of mouth marketing—you can only influence it.

Wouldn't you rather put this weapon of mass-influence—social media—to work **for** your business? While right now I am talking about your marketing strategies per se, this is still a discussion about the consumer-side of your online presence. As part of your customer-focused online presence you will be responding to complaints—and needing to respond faster than ever before.

As mentioned above, the activities of consumers in social media will continue with or without your participation. It **is** in the best interests of your business to enter into social media marketing, with a purpose and a strategy to execute that purpose. As outlined in this book, strategic participation in social media—where your target audience spends their time—allows you to influence how your business is perceived in addition to improving your sales.

A Social Media Marketing Example: Business Goes From Zero to Hero in 24 Hours

I'll share with you a great example of one customer's huge problem with a company, which transformed into an amazing "save" for the business because that company utilized social media channels and actively participated in those channels. This is a true story, shared at a marketing conference I attended: a bride-to-be orders her wedding dress online from a business in New York. Her wedding dress arrives but there is a problem with the dress—it is not the exact dress she ordered.

Our bride-to-be is distraught. The time difference prevents her from being able to call the business directly when she discovers the problem. Even if she does talk to them, returning the dress for a replacement won't help her. She lives in South Africa. Shipping the dress already took two weeks, and she doesn't have two more weeks to wait. Her wedding is sooner than that. Our bride shares her angst on the business' Facebook Fan Page, saying she ordered "x" dress for her wedding. She explains that she can't wear the dress that arrived, and it took two weeks just to get the dress to her in South Africa. Worse, she continues, her wedding takes place before she could possibly get a replacement.

The next morning in New York, an employee at the wedding dress shop who shares the responsibility of keeping tabs on their social media, sees our bride's distressed Facebook posting. The employee notifies the manager of the problem. The business is already checking their sales records to see if they can identify the customer by the information posted on their Facebook Page and work out a solution.

When the distraught bride-to-be does call, she is surprised by the business saying they were glad she contacted them. They had been working to identify her order, based on her posting to their Facebook Page. They explained that the Manager was waiting to speak with her personally. A few details were clarified and the exact dress she ordered is in stock. The Manager double checked the details of the dress and told our bride-to-be that the store would pay for immediate overnight delivery of this replacement dress to her.

This business having social media channels and being active in those channels, allowed the dress shop to turn one bride-to-be's nightmare into an unusually positive experience. There would have undoubtedly been more negative posts from this distraught customer, and other prospective customers would have been affected by her upset, as well as several 'sympathy posts' from other brides-to-be.

Our once distraught bride-to-be did end up writing several other postings. However, in this positive outcome, those posts were all very positive: how the business was expecting her call, was already working to solve her problem before she even spoke to them on the phone, and paid to have the replacement overnighted to her in South Africa. A woman scorned by a business was transformed into a woman understood and taken care of at a time when it mattered most. The business went from "Zero," potential "social media leper," to Hero inside of 24 hours!

Could the wedding dress crisis have had a positive outcome

without the business being involved in social media? For the bride-to-be . . . absolutely! But it wouldn't have had the over-the-top element of unexpected recognition from the dress shop, already working to solve her crisis before she could even call the business directly. And what would the outcome of this crisis have looked like for the business, were they not utilizing social media channels?

Well, if the bride-to-be was unable to share her upset on the dress shop's Facebook Page—her only after-hours access to that business—our distraught bride-to-be would have definitely released her angst somewhere else. As a matter of fact, she probably did post on her own Facebook profile and/or Twitter in addition to posting on the business' Facebook Page. From her perspective, she was in an emotional crisis and needed to 'vent'. If the dress shop didn't have a Facebook Page, the business would simply never have known about this bride-to-be's social media "venting."

Her very distraught call, several hours later when the shop was open, would have been the first they were made aware of her problem. The dress shop may still have taken impressive action to solve her crisis by shipping the replacement dress overnight, certainly a great relief for our bride-to-be. But if she was only relieved by the actions the dress shop took after her frantic call, she may not have been moved to go back to **all** of the social media channels she had "vented to," to update her social media followers on how the dress shop solved her crisis.

Because the business did have at least one social media channel, their Facebook Page, and because they pay attention to their Facebook Page, this customer reached a company expecting her to call, hoping she would contact them so they could verify who had placed the order and quickly get the correctly appointed dress to her in time for her wedding. This customer was made to feel valued, understood and cared for, as though her problem was indeed something the dress shop wished to solve quickly and accurately solely to relieve her anxiety.

This considerate response and acknowledgement from the business moved her to sing their praises when updating **all** of the social media channels she had "vented to." Telling everyone about the amazing way her crisis was solved by the dress shop, this bride-to-be's desire to share her amazing and positive story turned what started as impassioned negative "word of MOUSE" marketing into a blissfully satisfied customer praising that same business—**shortly after** her initial negative postings.

This is one example of how social media has a powerful impact on your business, whether or not your business utilizes it. Wouldn't you rather know what is being said about your business, so that you can respond to it? Having the opportunity to acknowledge customers who share how much they appreciate you, as well as establishing a dialogue, working toward solutions for those who are not satisfied!

The customer complaint mechanism has gone from postal mail to telephone, then to e-mail, and finally to social media. Depending on which business we're talking about, consumers may never be sure who actually reads their 'complaint' email, but now, we have arrived to . . . "I have a problem. I post it on social media and half the planet knows about it in 15 seconds." There is a whole different level of business going on out there.

You can stick your head in the sand and try to ignore these facts. Or you can acknowledge the brave new world that today's marketplace is, venture out into social media and take your business to a different level, actually benefiting your business and those who need your products/services by actively using "word of MOUSE."

Social media is not a fad; it is not going away. It's only going to get bigger, stronger, and more pervasive as time goes on. It's important for businesses to get out there and work effectively in this space—the space of greatest activity in today's marketplace.

How we should handle business, including marketing, can change. There are points in time that are tipping points. 2013 has been identified by a number of informed sources, including Forbes and Neilsen, as a tipping point for establishing a social media foundation. Social media is no longer a marketing , it has become a necessity for business growth. 2014 is almost upon us. **Now is**

the time to seriously examine social media and mobile marketing for your business and make an informed decision. Then act on your decision.

Businesses that actually get active in their own social media channels **now** will have a more powerful marketing foundation than businesses which continue to play the ostrich, with their heads in the sand for another year or two, hoping social media will go away. Forbes and Neilsen did not use the illustration of an ostrich with its head in the sand; that was my description. But you need to get your business out there into the social media space **now**, while you can still be considered an early adopter in today's marketplace.

Does Anyone Have Social Media Marketing Figured Out?

Is your argument for not actively participating in social media marketing that no one has really figured it out yet? That is true. No one has it **completely** figured out. However, it is important to realize, with the current speed of development of technologies, social media marketing, or any technology for that matter, will not be completely figured out before its next evolution/advancement.

Technology is a moving target. And that target moves faster now than it did even one year ago. These days, waiting for everyone to figure it out before you take the plunge will only leave your business out of the center of growth. Worse, you are still not benefiting from—"word of MOUSE"—"the fastest growing source of word of mouth marketing.

Even if it's not perfect, get out there as effectively as possible. Begin with a starting strategy then build up and improve that strategy. Whether or not you start participating in today's marketplace is going to make a difference between sink or swim for a lot of small businesses. And, more than you might realize, it will even make the difference for large businesses.

So, one more time: you cannot control word of mouth marketing but you can influence it. And word of mouth is, now, more "word of MOUSE," moving at lightning speed as more than

60% of people do their Web surfing and social media postings via cell phone or tablet. Also social media has a powerful effect on your business whether your business chooses to engage in it or not!

Have you started to see social media marketing differently yet? Can you see that choosing not to utilize social media and mobile marketing in your business is a bigger, and potentially more problematic, decision for your business than choosing to take the social media marketing plunge?

A Mobile Marketing Example: Making a Difference for Business in Record Time

Now let me share an example of mobile marketing making a difference for a small business. There was a small restaurant near my home that had great food. They had been in business for a number of years; owned by relatively young people excited that they were doing all this "social stuff" to promote their business. They had a Facebook page, a Twitter feed, a Website, and even an e-mail newsletter.

Unfortunately, there wasn't much happening on their Facebook page to engage any of their, also young, clientele. This restaurant was primed to have a lot of activity from their young clientele on Facebook but it just wasn't there. Looking at their Facebook Fan Page posts revealed several employee postings: "We're going to be open tonight," or "DJ so-and-so is here tonight," or "Don't forget! Tonight's karaoke night." Comments from anyone who was not an employee were rare. Facebook check-ins were even rarer.

They had an impressive, though mostly business-centered, Website. An email newsletter subscription, in place for several years, was mostly limited to family, friends, and employees. Their Twitter feed, at least, was pretty active on various event nights.

One day, I posed a mobile marketing idea to one of the owners. My ideas was for a V.I.P. program that was perfect for restaurants, and I explained, "I'll run this for you for eight weeks at no charge. I'll learn a great deal from how this works out in a real world test, and you'll have a free mobile marketing program for two months. At the end of the trial you can take ownership the database of program participants."

I would manage the expense of setting up the program, the fees for the technology and the several print marketing pieces for use in the restaurant, I explained. I shared that I believed they would see a spike in business within eight weeks. I also gave them the option to continue with the program as a paying client, at the end of the trial. This would include any adjustments that might prove necessary during the trial. All I needed from them was a place for the easel poster, placement for some table tents, inserts placed into their 'bill folders,' and a total for the mobile coupons that were redeemed each week, which they would manage via a special key assignment in their cash register.

There were six parts to this mobile program idea. I had a vision of it being a great program. However, sometimes reality doesn't match up to your vision. Your best plan can be great **until** it meets reality when "surprises" can happen. So, a real world test was to be my great "proving ground." The owners were excited about having a free marketing program but doubted anything particularly impressive was going to happen within eight weeks.

The restaurant had been getting some new customers each week with a Groupon, but hadn't seen any repeat business from this. When I re-illustrated how this program generated return business, the owners became more excited. Finally, we agreed on the roles each side would play during those eight weeks.

I put together a VIP program for the restaurant where people could send a text to a certain number and they would get an instant coupon for 15% off their bill for that visit and a coupon for the next time they came in. There were just under 200 people in that database in less than two and a half weeks.

I surveyed the VIP program participants at the middle of the third week via a virtual text conversation. For example, "Which coupon is your favorite? The restaurant could make changes to current coupons, essentially, on the fly. They could also broadcast news, such as, "Guess what? We're going to have so-and-so come and play live tonight!" or "Come on down to the Street Fair this Saturday and get a free appetizer!"

This was all delivered via text to participant cell phones. It could also go to email or only to email at the participant's discretion. This was not frequent, annoying texting. One coupon per week. There were also other ways restaurant customers could earn more coupons, while at the restaurant. Another survey, conducted within the last two weeks of the program revealed that participants did not want this program to end. The V.I.P. program had addressed something different for this business and allowed them a new level of engagement with their customers. Program participants were receiving multiple benefits from this program at no cost. There was more happening in the eight weeks of this little program than had happened with the restaurant's e-mail newsletter over several years. It was an impressive demonstration of results within a short period of time.

Clearly, just "having" social media doesn't mean it's working for you. Engaging in social media without an effective strategy is likely to only cost you time without yielding effective results. You can be productive or you can be busy. This business had been participating in their social media, but that participation was merely "busy work"—what they had been doing wasn't really productive.

Did I mention that all of this was from one piece of the six-piece program? I shared with you, our agreement as to what our respective roles would be during this trial program. Unfortunately, the restaurant did not keep up their side of the bargain. They didn't respond to the first survey results I provided to them. They could have adjusted a couple of the coupons to repeat the most popular coupons or try new ones. I tried to encourage the owners to allow me to generate a broadcast text to the program participants, to notify them of special offers the restaurant was running during a street fair that took place during the trial period. The owners never responded to emails, texts, or phone calls about creating a broadcast.

So, this one piece of the six-part program could have performed even better than it did. Additionally, the restaurant did not place the table tents and placed only a few bill-folder pieces into bill-folders. In essence, less than 10% of customers even knew about the benefits of posting a Facebook status or doing a Facebook check-in while at the restaurant. The program could have produced even greater results for the restaurant than the already impressive outcomes we realized.

Make Social Media a Game-Changer for YOUR Business

Social media is an incredible opportunity to reach more potential customers than you could possibly reach otherwise. As a small business owner, proper utilization and attention to social media channels appropriate for your business, is the single largest game-changing tool you could wield!

We know, that in addition to utilizing the Internet to research their purchases, consumers are influenced by "word of MOUSE." But is there growth within various social media channels that actually drives purchases? Let's talk about that. We'll use one of the newest comers, Pinterest and one that business owners usually consider the least worthy of their time—Twitter. According to Business Insider's recent BI Intelligence report, The New Art Of Social Commerce: How Brands And Retailers Are Converting Tweets, Pins, and Likes Into Sales, even though Pinterest has only one-fifth the number of users as Faceboook, Pinterest's impact on e-commerce is HUGE. They accounted for 23% of global social-mediated e-commerce sales in the second quarter of 2013, compared to a mere 2% just one year ago. And Twitter, yes Twitter, also over-performed accounting for a 22% share of sales. Are you beginning to see the value of incorporating social media into your business marketing?

One advantage that small businesses have over larger businesses, when it comes to utilizing social media marketing is that they can be more agile in their decision making. Small businesses don't have to weave through four to six committees before choosing to utilize a marketing strategy or modify a tactic within a strategy and put it into action.

We talked earlier about the wildly expansive rate at which social media can potentially move. Make social media marketing work for your business. Develop content-rich, customer-focused marketing messages. Deliver these messages via an interlaced social media marketing strategy appropriate for your business industry and business culture. This approach allows social media marketing to do more for your business growth than any other single methodology of marketing.

3

Why Retaining Control Of YOUR "Business Voice" In Your Social Media Is A Primary Business Survival Tactic

What is "Business Voice"?

First, let's acknowledge that to a certain extent "business voice" exists in the traditional, 'business-focused marketing.' You remember 'business-focused marketing'—the left-over standard of marketing—"Yes, our business is the best, forget the rest." It could also be said, though to a much smaller extent, that "business voice" has a presence in your marketing at all times.

That said, I coined the phrase "business voice" for the purpose of assigning a name, a recognizable label, to a problem I see over and over again in social media marketing. So, when I talk about "business voice" here, I am speaking only about content/information that businesses place in their social media channels, or that businesses outsource to others to place in their social media. Social media channels, meaning: blog postings, Facebook posts, comments, answers to questions posed on social media platforms, etc. I'm using the word "platform" here to refer to different manners of social media, e.g. Facebook, Facebook Groups, blogs, online video Website services, Pinterest, Twitter, LinkedIN, etc.

Why Do Business Owners Give Away Their Power . . . The Power of Their "Business Voice"?

Okay, now you have some reference for the terms I'll be using as we talk about the importance of your "business voice." Next, let me tell you, I have been asked by many business owners, marketers, speakers, and business professionals, to help get them started on Facebook and LinkedIN and "do" their Facebook and LinkedIN postings for them. Many of these business owners also ask, "There isn't a real reason we should be on Twitter, is there? Our market certainly does not include teenagers!" or "We hear several different answers when it comes to the recommended frequency of social media postings. Let's talk about having you handle that for our business."

One of the first things I say in response to these business owners is, "I'm happy to get your business set up and coach you on how to most powerfully manage your social media postings. I'm also happy to explain how to, almost painlessly, work social media marketing into your business operations." AND I add to that response that I won't do the postings for them, because I **strongly** believe that turning their "business voice" over to their social media savvy child, young adult niece, or a marketer, even a great marketer, is about the single worst business decision they could ever make. My response is about 180 degrees from what they expect I should say. They are usually under the impression that 'doing' social media postings is most of what my business does.

You may be thinking the same thing. However, I'm not like

most social media marketing consultants. I have a different approach to utilizing a social media presence. Remember what works is customer-focused marketing and nowhere is that **more** true than in social media. I believe the reasoning behind my 'seemingly strange response,' to the business owners I referred to above will make the most sense if I walk you through a few examples. These are examples of requests I have had from business owners wanting to hire me to help them with, or to take charge of, their social media. You might identify with one of these examples, which may help you 'anchor' the impact of "business voice" to your business situation.

This first example happens most often with very small and/or very new businesses. The business owner wants to "be out there" in social media. Even if they aren't convinced that social media is a true marketing tool, they want to "get out there" and just figure it out along the way. So, we discuss the price of developing a progressive, interlaced social media marketing strategy, matching their business culture. Setting them up in the appropriate social media channels, and then teaching key business personnel how to make the best use of those channels with the untapped resources they already have available in their business, adding that I would coach them on how to find those untapped resources. Then I would coach them on how to integrate this new marketing strategy into their regular business operations so they can emerge from my coaching able to continue, powerfully, on their own. This is what I **actually** do in my business.

Who Are You Trusting With Your "Business Voice"?

Now, if the result of this discussion with the business owner is more than they want to spend on social media marketing, the business owner will say, "Thanks, but that's' more than I want to spend on this thing. My teenage daughter/nephew/neighbor's college-age-son is great with social media, knows it inside out. I'll just hire him/her to do it. And I know I can hire them to do the postings."

So, what's wrong with this approach? I have no doubt that

their daughter/nephew/whatever IS probably an uncrowned Queen or King of the ins and outs of social media. They could probably post to social media in their sleep. And, just as likely, that person doesn't know the first thing about social media **marketing**, or any kind of marketing for that matter.

If the business owner chooses to hire a 'grass roots marketer,' for lack of a better term, will that business owner end up with a social media presence in the platforms he chooses, or is directed to choose? Absolutely! Is this a good example of social media marketing? NO! Is this a wise business decision? 98% of the time—No! I'm allowing a 2% possibility that the person they choose could be a marketing "natural." What is the result of this choice? This business owner has not actually saved marketing dollars on a new marketing strategy. He/She may have turned their business' fastest potential growth tool into a potential "fastest colossal failure tool," by turning his "business voice" over to someone who knows nothing, or next-to-nothing, about using social media as a marketing tool for business growth.

A second example: a business owner, with either a new or well-established business, is on-board with investing some of his/her marketing dollars to establish a good social media presence, wanting to 'stay in front of' these new, and growing, social media communities. The phrase "stay in front of" refers to being at the 'front' of the mind in one's target audience. In the case of social media, this tactic traditionally involves frequent, even very frequent, message postings to various social media platforms by a given business. This frequent 'exposure' to that business' brand and marketing message is intended to cause the potential customer to think of that business rather than any other when they are in need of a product or service.

The business owner in this example wants someone who understands business and marketing handling his social media, not just a social media-savvy young adult. This business owner also believes that the marketers should be managing the social media postings for them. Why? It could be:

- he/she doesn't want to invest the time/labor hours to manage social media postings

- he/she doesn't want to invest in training key personnel on how to manage the postings
- he/she believes that only marketers can manage posting effectively and wants to hire me to do that for him/her, feeling this is similar to hiring someone to manage his/her business advertising.

Or, this business owner is seeing social media as another chore that has to be done and not as the opportunity for game-changing growth that it is. When I talk about why I won't do social media postings for my customers, the business owner is confused, assuming that is where I should be making my money—from the repeating fees for ongoing social media postings.

This business owner either tries to convince me to do his social media postings or believes that telling me that he/she will take their business elsewhere unless I do the postings, will convince me to agree to his/her requests. I 'stick to my guns' and decline to do the postings. I share my reasoning with him/her.

The business owner does not want to have anyone in his business manage postings. He definitely wants to hire a marketer to do his postings, so we part ways, wishing each other luck. He shops on for another social media marketer who wants to be hired to do the postings as well as establish the social media presence for this business owner.

Final example: a business owner with a 12-year old business is ready to "go social!" He asks me to "build him one of those cool Facebook Pages so he can discover new people to talk to about his business." He just wants me to create the Facebook Page for him; he does not want any coaching on how to use the Facebook Page or ideas for how to 'market' with it. He does not even want to explore other, potentially more suitable social media channels for his business. He just wants me to build the Page and he will take care of his own postings and self-training. This business owner can't understand why I turn down his offer of business.

In each of these examples, I turn down their business for the same basic reason. The business owner is choosing an ineffective use of social media for their business marketing. They are: ignoring the need for strategy, choosing tactics for having social media but not establishing social media marketing, or are attaching to a strategy that will most likely not produce any "bank-able" results. None of these examples is looking for, or is open to, a social media marketing **consultant**.

What if I did create what the above business owners asked for, the way they asked for it? When their social media plan fails to have "bank-able" results, their poor results would reflect badly on my business. After all, I am the Social Media Consultant, it must have been my idea to do it that way and that plan failed.

No, thank you! I am in the business of helping small businesses **grow** their business. When I help a small business improve their Website traffic, increase conversion of prospects to leads and leads into paying customers who become return customers, my own business looks great! That's what I'm interested in.

Two of the above examples are not only ready to turn over their business voice to me, they want me to **be** their business voice. Then the one example who actually wants to manage his own social media postings, doesn't seem to have a realistic plan for thier 'voice'.

One Scenario of Losing Your "Business Voice"

Let me share one more thing with you. Let's see if you can define "business voice" for yourself . . . before I tell you. I believe the concept will be even stronger for you, if you figure it out before I explain. Here goes . . .

Let's say your business is the proud, new owner of a presence on a few different social media platforms. You now have a Facebook Fan Page, a LinkedIN profile, your Website designer added a blog to your Website, and you even decided to start a Twitter account . . just in case there's a way to work it into your strategy.

"Word of MOUSE"—Today's "Word of Mouth" Marketing

Let's say you hire a marketer to do your Facebook postings or blog postings for you. Even in the unlikely event that marketer knew everything there is to know about what you do in your business, there is no way that the words, phrases, or descriptions he/she puts into your postings would sound like someone who is invested-in, vastly knowledgeable, or **passionate** about that information.

If **you** create those posts, it's going to have an entirely different feel for the person reading it. You may argue that your target audience doesn't know who is actually writing the posts. However, you'd be surprised. Once they have read a few posts or asked a question through one of your social media platforms, they are going to know whether the person on the other side of this virtual conversation truly understands your business. If it's just some stranger creating posts and answering questions, or trying to answer questions, your customers **will** know.

Say you actually get activity on your Facebook page and/or your blog, because you are re-developing your marketing messages from the perspective of your target audience. If that activity is answered by a marketer, someone who is not attached to or lacks understanding of your business, you could easily lose that prospective customer.

Why? Something brought that prospect to your online information. That prospect came to your business for answers to their questions or solutions to their problems. Now, when they are taking that next step with your business, developing a relationship with your business by following your Facebook or blog posts, they are not met with the manner of information that brought them to you. Instead, they are finding content that is more like every other business. Content that does not demonstrate an understanding of their needs and problems.

Then what happens when they ask a question on your Facebook Page or blog—who would answer it? The marketer? Does the marketer **know** the answer? What if you, or someone deeply familiar with **your** business, was managing your own social media content? Your answer to that question could be the beginning of your next, most loyal, and repeat, customer. Am I painting an effective picture for you?

Whether it's a blog article, answering a question on your Facebook Fan Page/Group, a response to a prospect's comment on your blog, or a response to a question from your Twitter feed, how the words in those postings/responses are strung together when written, the phrases chosen and the knowledge and insight, or lack thereof, **IS** your "business voice."

The postings which a marketer, even a great marketer, writes may be well structured and contain information. They may, or may not, be engaging. That would be one expression of a "business voice." In this example, **your** business voice. How strong? How engaging? How knowledgeable? How informative? How **invested** . . . is this example of your "business voice"?

Your business voice should be one of your highest valued resources. And if your business voice is your most highly valued resource, who do you believe should be in control of it? Do you want a vested and knowledgeable voice, a contrived voice, a passionate voice? What kind of voice do you want as the ambassador of your business? Who should be the source of that voice?

Remember the example of the bride-to-be and her wedding dress? What different outcome might there have been if that dress shop had someone else managing their social media postings? Would the person in charge of the dress shop's social media have waited to create a response, until they had gotten in touch with the dress shop directly?

Would they have created some response for the bride-to-be while they worked to get in touch with the dress shop? What would that response have been? Would their response to the bride-to-be have been something the dress shop would have said? Would that response have been a positive or a less-than-positive portrayal of the dress shop? How long would it have taken for them to contact the dress shop? Would they have called the dress shop or emailed the dress shop? What if a comparable situation had happened in your business?

Earlier we discussed the history of marketing and communication over the last several decades. Citing that gone are the days of two-plus weeks of turn-around-time when responding to a customer concern or complaint by postal mail. Going are the days when you would just receive a phone call from an upset customer. It's no longer even an upset email. We have become a society focused on instant, or nearly instant, gratification or recourse. And when it comes to the mobility of engaging in social media these days, technology has risen to the occasion. If a customer is upset they may choose to share that response via Facebook, Twitter, consumer blog, or online customer review. OR all of the above! Shouldn't your business put its "best **voice** forward"? Who else is going to care more about your business than you, the business owner? Or at least, people within your business who understand your business as well as its culture? **Now**, ask yourself, who is the best choice to be the "voice of my business"?

HOT TIP

Your business voice should be one of your highest-valued resources. If your business voice is your most highly valued resource, who do you believe should be in control of it?

Choosing YOUR business to be Your "Business Voice"

The postings you would write may, or may not, be well structured. However, your posts can definitely have the possibility of containing more than mere information. They can be informative **and** insightful. Add to that how much more you know about your business than any marketer—the knowledge, the wisdom, the insights, the tips, the tricks. When you have a business, your business is important to you. It is, at least, your livelihood and, quite possibly, your passion. Together, these things make the **most powerful** "business voice." You, as business owner, are the most powerful voice for your business.

The next best thing is when that business voice is in the hands of one, or more, individuals **in** your business. Individuals who are well-versed in not only what your business does, but how your business does business—the 'culture' of your business. Your business is important to your employees; it is their livelihood. And you want to create relationships with your target audience, your potential future customers. Individuals within your business can share an authentic voice for your business because they are involved in your business. You may have some employees who are very passionate about their jobs/about your business, unlike any outsourced individual or company.

One time, I went against my own principle of not doing social media postings for someone else. I wanted to help a friend with a new line of business. They had received special recognition for this new environmentally conscious and very clever product, and I wanted to help them get their message out to a wider audience while that recognition and the media pieces that came with it were still fresh.

I was well informed on the details of this new line of business and very excited about the clever products. I established a couple of social media channels, including a Facebook Fan Page. I developed a following for this new line, among some like-minded businesses, organizations and individuals. There were postings about events and new product resource arrivals, which had interesting or celebrated histories. I actually needed more input from the business than I was getting to provide interesting content more frequently and attract more fans fairly quickly. This would result in this new Fan Page showing up in front of more people.

It might sound like a good plan to have an outsourced someone, who is well-informed about a business, create social media postings that make sense and sound engaging. But, it really isn't a good plan. It's when a prospect asks a question online that the outsourced-social-media-posting-person doesn't know the answer to, that the business owner can truly appreciate the value of a rather immediate feedback loop!

The outsourced-social-media-posting-person, in this case me, needs to get in touch with the business to provide a reply to a question. The question was from a person who was traveling when they saw this Facebook Fan Page. I'll say they were traveling from the Midwest. That isn't exactly true, but the person was essentially halfway across the country.

They were already on their way to Southern California. Upon discovering the Facebook Fan Page, they actually wanted to make an appointment to meet on the business site and talk about special ordering a number of these products. This was someone who needed to have a dialogue with the business owner, or manager. They didn't know that I am not someone in that business.

I called the business phone. No one answers and I get voicemail. It is slightly after hours, but the question is time sensitive, so I try a personal number and get another voicemail. I leave voice messages at both numbers and send an e-mail to all of the email addresses I have for them, business and personal, and wait for an answer the next morning.

I try calling again the next morning. Still only voicemails. The business address and phone number are available on the Fan Page. However, the Fan Page itself is supposed to be a manner of business contact. This person was not just a prospect. This individual wanted to be a customer.

What is wrong with this situation? 1) I, not being someone in the business, could not answer the customer's question. Even though I really wanted my business owner to know about this as soon as possible, not only as a client, but as a friend. 2) Working long hours to manage a couple of project deadlines, the business was deferring phone calls and emails for a period of time 3) There had also been a change in the personal cell phone number that I wasn't made aware of.

The not-great result: this prospect who wanted to be their customer, did not hear back from the business in a timely manner. Had the business owner been doing their own social media postings, they could have replied as soon as they saw that question posted! Who knows how much business was lost in this instance?

What else can we learn from this example? 1) In this particular instance, the business owner may not have seen the post even had they been doing their own social media, since they were deferring communications to meet a project deadline. So, even if a business is doing their own social media postings if they aren't paying attention to their social media this sale would still have been lost. 2) If the business doesn't provide dates of upcoming events or points of interest about the business, your outsourced-social-media-posting-person can't provide the best postings on behalf of your business even if they truly care about your business. I believe a large part of this dis-connect of information for postings coming from a business is due to #3. 3) Having someone else "do" the social media for your business has the undesired effect of the business owner distancing him/herself from providing information to their outsourced personnel, which could help their social media postings shine. This distancing yourself from your own business voice is not at all good for your business.

If the business owner were managing their own social media, notifications could have been set up to arrive via e-mail or go to their cell phone and make the business owner aware that someone had posted to their Facebook Page. Armed with a smartphone, that business owner could have seen the questions posted and seeing how important the posting was, answered it in less than a minute! Bang! They could have quickly set up an appointment to meet that hot prospect at their business and made an amazing sale. This was an unnecessary loss of business!

Business IS Personal

An often overlooked reality of business is that people do business with other people, not with businesses. For eons, we have worked at separating our personal stuff from our business stuff. Yet, all this time it has been the personal aspect to doing business that really matters. Just recall a time when you had dealings with a business. A time when one, or more, individuals in that business mis-handled your business dealings. Whether it was an end-product, a financial aspect, or a point of contract, what, in your mind, matters most about the dealings with that business now? The business or the people in that business? . . . the people! "Business IS personal." Extremely personal, actually. And personal matters.

People do business with the people in a business, more than with the actual business. Businesses are entities; things that exist. Businesses have their technologies; they have their processes. But it's the people in a business that make that business different from another business.

It's the people within a business who decide what processes are going to be utilized, what tenets/principles are to be important. Whether that business will be great and serve their customers, or just get customers for long enough that they realize they need another business which actually wants to help them—it's the people who decide. "What tech are we going to use and how are these processes going to be executed? Are we going to put processes in place to assure we are taking proper care of our customers?" All of these questions come back to the people. The customers, the prospects, the company management and company employees—they're all people!

Viver Winters Israel

4

Where to Find Untapped Treasures Of Content For Your Social Media That Already Exist Within Your Business

How Will I Find Time to Create Social Media Content?

At this point, you're probably thinking, "Okay. I get that this could be important to do. Maybe I should be doing this but I don't have time. I'm already overwhelmed. How am I supposed to find any time to create social media content? This is just something else I'm going to have to deal with. Which of my other business responsibilities am I going to 'not do' to make time for creating content for these blog posts, for Facebook, and for videos. Seriously, videos! Who has time to shoot videos?"

How? First, let's focus on utilizing the hidden treasures of content already available in your business! Then we will look at the rest of the magic of "finding" that time when we get to Chapter 6.

Where to Find YOUR Hidden 'Content Treasures'

There are many hidden treasures of content within your business, just waiting to be discovered! How many questions have customers or potential customers asked you, or one of your employees, over the years? That is content! Think of all of the customer service questions. That is content. Think of the complaints from customers. That is content. Have you been keeping any kind of record of those questions? Get that record! It's content! If one person had a question about something, others are likely to have the same question.

Instead of answering each customer query as if it were only that individual's concern, consider that there are probably many other individuals who have the same question. These are some of the treasure content pieces for your blog, which can answer those question for many people. When they go searching for the answer to that question, oh boy! Do you already have a list of frequently asked questions? That is also content. If you don't have a list of frequently asked questions (FAQs), that is another item for your Marketing To-Do List.

It's all content! And phrased properly, it's going to be solving your target audience's problems and questions. First, since it's already been a customer's concern, maybe not a problem, but certainly a concern, question or a need, you know it's relevant. That's content in all of those e-mails, so go through them. What questions have come in? These are answers you should provide. Memos that have gone back and forth within the company also deserve a look. There may be usable content there as well.

Just in how you do what you do in your business, there is a huge amount of content. Take the example of River Pools and Spas in Virginia. They had frequent questions being asked about the pools they built? So, they made basic, no-frills videos of the different aspects of their pool-building process. As well as posting FAQs, such as, "How do you build and in-ground pool?" "How do you build an above ground pool?" "Which is better? Do you build your pool in sand or build it in gravel?"

How to Make the MOST of Each Piece of Content

Take each one of your questions and make it a blog post. Then make it a video. Then add that question to the FAQ area on your Website. Consider stripping the audio from your video and making that a podcast. Or, if you aren't up to making short videos, simply record yourself stating a question, then answering that question and make that a podcast.

Focus on one question, or concern, at a time in your article/blog post. Answer that question/concern in each of the learning methods: reading, hearing, seeing and when possible, with how-to videos, for those who learn by watching or doing. Each media should have all the keywords that are appropriate to that one question/concern. That is going to be search engine candy for your business. And you haven't paid for AdWords or search engine optimization!

HOT TIP

Focus on one question, or concern, at a time in your article/blog post. Answer that question/concern in each of the learning methods: reading, hearing, seeing and when possible, with how-to videos, for those who learn by watching or doing. Each media should have all the keywords that are appropriate to that one question/concern.

People like to learn in different ways; visual, kinesthetic (doing), auditory are only a few. There are many studies on how people learn. Some individuals learn more effectively by reading information, while others learn most effectively if they hear the information. Still others learn by physically doing a task.

You want to speak to all the potential audiences, because you don't know which is their favorite learning method. So, provide your content in multiple different medias! The more types of media you utilize for publishing your marketing information, the larger the audience you will appeal to. This makes your information more accessible to your target audience. One question, one issue, answered via many different media.

Often, when you're in the process of putting these hidden treasures into content as a blog post, video, etc., other topics will come to your mind. You think, "Oh, yeah, that reminds me of something one potential customer asked me." Or, "That reminds me of a question I believe customers should ask but never do."

These "**should** ask" questions (SAQs) are also very powerful to have online as specific content pieces. Make them a featured series: "Questions Pool Shoppers Should Ask!"—Your Featured Question." These pieces may not have the same search engine candy effect as your frequently asked questions, but when people start coming back to you, finding what they need at your site, they're going to start looking at what else you have and they will find these questions.

Posting these "SAQs" further empowers your target audience to make good choices, decisions and/or avoiding painful mistakes. They're going to love you for it and become raving fans of your business. Then what will your target audience do with those questions? They will share them on their social media. They may also share them in online customer review sites.

This content doesn't just go out there and disappear. Maybe someone who has held on to your business card, the classified ad, the newspaper ad or your direct mail piece, will contact your business at a future date. However, content placed online lives on 24 hours a day/7 days a week/365 days a year. As time goes on, and more people share it, that information continues to serve your business not just as one retained business card, classified ad or direct mail piece but as a massive, living source of information and referral!

Now, when you get emails from customers asking questions, answer those questions in a blog post or FAQ and post it to your Website. Reply to that email, thanking your customer for their question. Let them know that their question was valuable; tell them you wrote an article about their question/concern and posted it to your Website. Then give them a link to that article, which answers their question. Now, each time you answer a customer/prospect concern you are increasing your status as an expert in your field, building relationships with your customers and target audience. You are establishing trust, making those answers available to all who may need the information, brining more people to your Website. You'll get more bang for your buck with each customer/prospect interaction that you have in your business from this point forward. How cool is that?

Worksheet: My Possible Sources for Content Treasures

☐ Questions Customers Have Asked by Phone

☐ Concerns Customers Have Called In

☐ Complaints Customers Have Called In

☐ Questions Customers Have Asked by Email

☐ Concerns Customers Have Emailed In

☐ Complaints Customers Have Emailed In

☐ Questions Posted on Your Social Media

☐ Concerns Posted on Your Social Media

☐ Complaints Posted on Your Social Media

☐ Information in Company Memos

☐ Frequently Asked Questions From Other Sources

☐ Questions You Know Customers Should Ask But Don't

☐ _____

☐ _____

☐ _____

☐ _____

5

Where to Start: Making Sense of Social Media & Which Types are Appropriate for YOUR Business

Now you're thinking, "I'm still trying to get a picture here of which social media I should be involved in." If this sounds familiar, pay close attention to this chapter. Jot down questions and thoughts you may have as you read. Doing so for both Chapters 5 and 6 will help identify which media types/channels make the most sense for your business when beginning your social media marketing campaign.

Getting Familiar With The Most Effective Types of Social Media for Your Business

You are searching for the two, or three, social medial channels that seem best-suited for your business and your business culture.

As you consider your choices, focus on what matters most for your business. Once you've made your choices, number those choices in order of importance.

Generally, I wouldn't suggest starting with more than three new channels of social media marketing. It is more powerful to begin with incorporating a couple of channels into your regular business operations and becoming comfortable with those, before adding additional marketing channels. You can always add another channel, or two, later on. After reading this chapter, review the thoughts and questions you've written down. Then re-read Chapter 5 to add any more thoughts or questions, as well as eliminating any which are no longer relevant.

What <u>Exactly</u> is Social Media?

Isn't social media just Facebook, LinkedIN, and Twitter?
No! There is a great deal more to social media than many people realize. Social media is not just Facebook, Twitter, and LinkedIn. YouTube is social media. Online customer review sites, such as Yelp, are social media. Blogs are social media. Online directories, which may have a component for online customer reviews, are social media. Pinterest, a relatively new and very visually driven platform, is also social media. And Instagram, while it may not **seem** very applicable to business, is still social media and is growing rapidly.

In this book, we are only going to address those most popular and most effective types (channels and platforms) of social media. These are the social media offerings that matter most when your interest is not simple social media, but social media marketing. As a marketer for your business, you want to BE where most your target audience IS. You could drive yourself crazy trying to be on even just 30% of the social media sites that are 'out there,' so it makes more sense to focus on those channels which can give you the most bang for your business buck. And when I say, "buck," I am also referring to the **time** you "spend" on your social media. Time, after all, is one of your most valuable assets.

I'm going to begin with those social media channels with which you might be less familiar, instead of those you may know best. This is to inspire you to read about those, possibly less familiar, channels that you might otherwise automatically dismiss from your thinking. Even if one, or more, of the channels presented here seem as though they couldn't possibly be of any value to your business, please read about **each** channel presented. This is an exercise in exploration and discovery. For the purpose of increasing your business' bottom line, it's worth your time to read and consider each one.

Let's imagine that you think Twitter is the last thing on earth you would ever consider as a serious marketing tool. Please, read the information about Twitter **anyway**. Reading about Twitter, here, is just between you and your copy of this book. It can be a secret. This book won't share your secret with anyone.

After reading the examples, you might surprise yourself with what comes to mind for **your** business. If you don't find anything worthy for your business after reading about Twitter, no one ever has to know you read about Twitter. But . . . what if you do have an inspiring thought after reading the Twitter examples? If that's the case, wouldn't you be glad you invested that time reading about silly, old Twitter?

Pinterest—More Important for Business Than Most People Realize!

I'm going to start our discussion with Pinterest. Now, you may already be very aware of Pinterest. But . . . did you know that Pinterest is, interestingly, **very** commercial friendly? There are actually several possibilities for working Pinterest into your business: increasing exposure and maybe directing people to your Facebook Fan Page from your Pinterest Page, or better yet, having them see your Pinterest items **from** your Facebook Fan Page, **then** taking prospects to your Website from your Pinterest Page!

Pinterest is an excellent channel for a business to utilize for social media marketing. It's fresh! Yes, it is fairly new, but it has exhibited an impressive ability to out-attract and out-perform other highly established social media channels, especially with respect to marketing. Pinterest is not going away any time soon. Is it experimental? You could say so, yes. But for that matter, Facebook is still experimental.

It wasn't long ago that Facebook went public (going from existing as a privately held company to a company being publicly held and traded on a Stock Exchange). Once it did "go public," it actually entered a whole new realm of business, because, **now**, Facebook needed to satisfy many more stockholders.

Facebook was changing things left and right within a fairly short timeframe before they "went public." Even more frequent changes came about after "going public." Social media is amazing and important to your business, but no business should have all of its "social media marketing eggs" in one basket—especially if that "basket" is under someone else's control.

HOT TIP

Social media is amazing and important to your business. But no business should have all of it's "social media marketing eggs" in one basket, especially if that "basket" is under someone else's control.

But back to Pinterest for your social media marketing! Pinterest is VERY visual. One of the primary components to enjoying success for your business with Pinterest marketing is the creation of engaging visual items, called "pins," on your Pinterest Page. Hum-drum, text-heavy "pins," with poor graphic impact are not going to attract people's attention. And there are many, many attractive "pins" on Pinterest which do attract attention; those pins are the ones your "pins" will be competing with.

One great use of Pinterest for any type of business, is to further market a podcast. If you have, or end up planning to have, a podcast for your business, create a "board" on your Pinterest Page for your podcast. Have a graphic artist, or someone you know who is good with image generating software, create a variation of your podcast cover art. A variation that you adjust for each podcast episode. This allows you to still 'brand' your podcast cover art and have the title of each podcast episode show more predominately then it might in the cover art for your podcast show. Consider adding multiple color backgrounds, which you rotate through over several episodes, to build more visual interest in your Pinterest 'podcast board.'

Have each "pin" for your specific podcast episodes link directly to your blog; to the very podcast/blog post where that podcast episode 'lives'! (You can have this done via a WordPress plugin called "PowerPress.") Voila! Someone looking around on the INCREDIBLY highly visited Pinterest site notices the "pin" for one of your podcast episodes, and thinks, "Oh, I'm interested in that!" They click on your "pin" and have now linked directly to that podcast episode on **your** Website (not just a link to your podcast show.)

By creating a visually interesting "pin" on Pinterest, you now have something not just of interest for your target audience but a marketing piece which can turn into a commercial win for you! Pinterest experienced an 88% growth rate over last twelve months, prior to the release of this book! Smile! This is **good** news!

Now, create a separate "pin" for each one of your podcast episodes, switching the background color and text for each episode title. It's most likely you will have more traffic from individuals being attracted to the content of a particular episode than to your podcast show overall. This strategy is definitely worth your time.

Think . . . what else does your business have that you could create a visually intriguing "pin" for? A book? A product? A service? A program? The demographic of individuals, predominately female, who frequent Pinterest love to buy! Do not underestimate Pinterest when it comes to choosing powerful social media marketing channels for your business. I made that mistake and I was wrong. Pinterest is GREAT for social media marketing! The biggest difference from other social media channels being it is driven by visual images: in Pinterest, visual interest RULES!

What About Google+ ?

Many people may disagree with my opinion of Google+. For a period of time, LOTS of people were very excited about Google+, and there are some fine features. At the same time, a number of their 'social' features are far from seamless or intuitive. In its present form, I don't see it becoming the be-all end-all that many people believed it would.

Is Google+ huge? Yes. Per GlobalWebIndex.net, Third Quarter 2013 Report, Google+ is catching up to Facebook in raw number of users. But that statistic is more a function of the fact that creating a Google+ account is mandatory when you sign up for a Google G-mail account. Meanwhile, no one **has** to create a Facebook account, so that "raw number of users" statistic is not a fair measure of desirability. Here, we are interested in intuitive usability for social sharing and usability in business marketing, not solely on volume of users. Remember, this is only my opinion.

I have spoken with business owners who are willing to put up with the non-intuitive workings of Google+ to have the features they do value, including Google Hangout. There are a lot of smart people at Google so I doubt they are done working to improve Google+.

Should I Use LinkedIN for Marketing?

Business owners often ask about LinkedIN. So let's talk a little bit about LinkedIn:
1. How is serious business done there?
2. How can I leverage it?
3. How do I use LinkedIN as a social media platform?

It is important to remember that users on LinkedIN are other business owners, entrepreneurs and business professionals. Human Resource personnel especially LOVE LinkedIN. It is a great resource to search for potential, specialized employee candidates and shop for middle/upper management candidates.

Realize also, there are a lot of individuals on LinkedIN looking for employment. Still others are looking for clients.

Before considering LinkedIN as a primary social media marketing platform, ask yourself, "Are these people my target audience?" If your business is a B2B business, meaning your clients are other businesses rather than individuals, LinkedIN could be a good platform for you. If your business is a B2C business, a business which provides products/services for individuals, ask yourself, "Are these people my target audience?"

If LinkedIN is full of your target audience, it can be a good choice, IF you actually visit LinkedIN frequently **and** participate. You could start a LinkedIN Group, since operating a LinkedIN group is a good point of credibility on LinkedIN. You could also shop through existing LinkedIN groups, reviewing the group descriptions, for groups that would serve your target LinkedIN audience. Asking yourself, is there something missing from what these groups offer? Is there something I could offer, in the form of discussion/information, that has been missed by other groups? LinkedIN, similar to Facebook, has both open groups (where anyone can join) and closed groups (where you need to ask to join and have your request to join accepted/declined by someone who 'administrates' that group).

However, I wouldn't recommend positioning it as one of your core marketing tools, unless LinkedIN is a treasure trove of **your** target audience. Your plan would have to include being attentive to LinkedIN, participating in groups, perhaps seriously considering establishing your own group. Even then don't make it one of your first choices. Many people believe it's the only serious place for business referrals to happen, but that really isn't true.

People are more relaxed when they're on Facebook. They're more relaxed when they're talking on a blog. More often than not, people seem to feel a need to speak "company speak" when they're 'talking' on their LinkedIN page or in LinkedIN groups. This lessens the very personal connection possible in LinkedIN conversations.

Yes, business can be done on LinkedIN. There are business professionals who focus primarily on LinkedIN for referrals as well as learning about other companies they need.

However, to illustrate why I don't believe LinkedIN is necessarily a good core choice for social media marketing, allow me to share some insight. A common mistake which many blog authors make is writing articles which attract other individuals in their industry. Why is this a problem? Those other individuals in their industry are not part of that business blog's target audience. Writing content which attracts your business' competition is not a good marketing strategy—they will rarely, if ever, buy from you or sing your praises to family, friends and co-workers. The point is to market to your target audience, not to your business industry, unless an aspect of your business industry IS your target audience. If you are a business owner who is grappling with how to effectively manage having a social media marketing program, LinkedIN may be the last channel you should use.

Can Twitter Really be Used as a Serious Marketing Tool?

Why would any serious business consider Twitter to be an actual marketing tool? It's true that a lot of what gets "tweeted" back, forth and around, by the predominately young people on Twitter, is ridiculous stuff that means very little while it's being typed, let alone after it's been "published." That said, such behavior is only one manner of use for Twitter. Make no mistake, Twitter has a place in business. There are great creative business uses for Twitter. And yes, I do have examples of businesses that make sales via Twitter. There are even business directories for Twitter. So, yes, there are businesses successfully using Twitter as a serious marketing tool, creating short marketing messages which 'speak' to the needs and problems of their target audience.

Twitter can really be quite an asset for short back and forth conversations in certain industries, such as construction companies, where personnel are always in the field. These personnel can expedite short communications via Twitter with smartphones instead of with a computer, via email, or by having to take the time for voice-to-voice phone calls.

Twitter for Speakers

Twitter has special value for individuals who do platform speaking as part of their business, or corporate personnel who move around a small, or large, region, to speak on corporate topics. Speakers can use Twitter to spare themselves as well as their audiences, the hassle of carrying notes and heavy handouts for presentations. For instance, let's say you were a platform speaker. Now, if the thought of public speaking makes you feel ill, don't worry—we are only pretending here. This is just to illustrate a point.

Imagine yourself as a brilliant speaker. You step up to the podium to deliver your speech. Before starting your speech, you share with your audience—by PowerPoint slide, easel board, etc.—a code for them to "Tweet" to a Twitter account, to get the Web address for a download of the PowerPoint presentation, notes and any additional materials. These would be sent directly to their phones. You can say to your audience, "You don't have to worry about carrying around your paper handouts or an enormous binder of [this presentation], because the link for all of that information has just been sent to your phone."

Now, they can focus on what you are saying instead of feverishly striving to take notes. Any slides and important information will be in the materials they receive by Tweet. For those in your audience who don't have smartphones, you also display the Web address for them to write down. But for those with smartphones, they don't have to write down anything! It gets better. You now have the cell phone number of everyone at your presentation who requested the materials! Tah-dah! Now, what are your thoughts about silly old Twitter?

Another plus here is that your PowerPoint presentations can be less cluttered. You have any important information detailed: charts, Web addresses, email addresses, phone numbers, all included as a digital handout in an information packet. Your audience doesn't have to write down what might be a very long web address just to go check out some cool resource you mentioned. It's all in the packet you prepared for them to receive via Twitter.

Or, say the manner of speech is not one where you want to provide a PowerPoint slide and notes handout. You can say, "If you would like to have this checklist of _____ which we have been discussing just tweet "Cklist" to @MyTwitterAccount, and the Web address (URL) will be delivered right to your phone.

Twitter—Life's Blood for Food Trucks

There is one industry that is almost Twitter-dependent. Food trucks have really embraced Twitter as a marketing tool, to let their customers know their exact location on a given day and range of time. Want to know where your favorite food truck is going to be on your days off? Subscribe to their Twitter feed. Let's say your friend has been raving about a food truck he discovered a couple of weeks ago. Want to find out where that food truck is going to be on your next day off? Check their Twitter feed.

The mobility of the food truck industry benefits enormously from Twitter as a marketing tool. Food truck with good food + Twitter feed can be a recipe for real success. Say your family is at Fitness Expo, or Brides Expo, or a Car or Boat Show. In addition to the food inside the Convention Center, there are several food trucks across one, or more, patio areas outside. One of these trucks has a menu that really captures your attention. You order something and it tastes great. You share on Twitter and/or Facebook, "Just ate at WhatABurger Food Truck; the food's amazing! They're at the ___ Expo through 5:00 PM Sunday." You'd be surprised how much activity can begin from a message like that. There are many food truck businesses which became success stories by their use of Twitter. Food truck owners LOVE Twitter!

Twitter Brings Crowds to a New Business Within 3 Hours

I also have a 'power of Twitter' example for a movie theater. When the Batman movie, *The Dark Knight*, first released, there was a theatre near my home which ended up opening almost two weeks ahead of schedule. The theater wasn't merely under new ownership, it was newly constructed, a beautiful, state of the art facility, including amazing sound systems, two theaters specially appointed for 3-D and an IMAX theater.

Hardly anyone knew about this place. I had been waiting for it to open to check it out but had yet to learn of its opening day. As I later learned from the owner, the place was nearly empty during its first week. The day that *The Dark Knight* released marked two weeks that the theater had been open, with essentially zero customers beyond some friends and family of those who worked there. This was because no one knew it was there.

I had the time to go see the film the day it released. However, being a hotly awaited release, all the showings for decent or relatively decent screening times were already sold out by that Friday morning. There were no screenings available until the next day. I decided to grab an early dinner at a favorite diner across from this new theater location. Then—surprise—the theater was open and showing *The Dark Knight* with **no one there**.

No lines around the building and down the stairs. I mean there were literally only three teenagers outside. I heard them talking, "Is everybody already inside?" "No." "You mean there's nobody here?" Then they started tweeting!

I walked over to the theater and talked to the man at the front door, who turned out to be the owner. I shared my surprise that they were open. He told me of their opening ahead of schedule so they could show *The Dark Knight* when it released, but their marketing wasn't changed in time. I asked him if he knew that his theater was the only one in a rather wide area that had available seating for *The Dark Knight*? I pointed out that "tons" of people are trying to find a place to see this film but can't get in, since there are no tickets available until the next day. He knew, but was at a loss for what else he could do about it; due to the late change in their opening date, they were even missing from movie listings both in newspapers and online.

I told him about the three teenagers I had seen tweeting about his theater having lots of available seating for *The Dark Knight*, adding that I would do the same. He was an older gentleman and didn't some to know what I was talking about. I didn't try to explain. I went inside, tweeted and posted on Facebook the treasure that I had happened onto. I was watching *The Dark Knight* in Imax! Mine was not a private screening, but I could have run all around in that theater and no one would have noticed.

When I came out of that showing the lobby was full and the queue lines for the cashiers were out the doors of the building. There were even two lines of people extending clear across the shopping venue, tickets in-hand, waiting to be let into that theatre for the next showings of *The Dark Knight*. It was the only place you could get in. That theatre had literally been put on the map within a two and a half hour period.

Seeing this **enormous** change, I looked for the Owner. I asked, "Do you know what happened here?" He said, "Well, I've got a lot of kids out there." I, again, told him what myself and the three teens had done when we realized there was no one at this newly opened theater, showing the movie that was sold out everywhere else. I explained, "All those kids came here because of Twitter."

When I went to a movie at that theater the following Friday, this man had a Twitter feed and counter posters with QR codes for coupons. He even had QR codes on bookmark flyers. He was doing all kinds of social media marketing now! Twitter made a huge difference for his business, before he even knew what it was. Twitter was his new best friend!

Selling Computers via Twitter

Over several years, Dell, Inc. (Computer company) sold thousands upon thousands of computers via Twitter. Granted, this was among a predominately school-age demographic. Still, they did generate a significant amount of income through Twitter, serving an important portion of their target audience. Of late, Dell may no longer be the greatest example of a rising star, as they have "filed" to be taken off the Stock Exchange. They want go back to being a privately-held company. Things are happening in the desktop computers/laptop computer market, and sales aren't what they used to be. So much has shifted to mobile technology—iPads/tablets and smartphones—which is, indeed, part of what we are talking about in this book.

Dell's example, however, absolutely speaks to the point that getting engaged in social media is all the more important due to social media engagement also being driven by the mobile device boom. Remember, in Chapter One I said, "In today's marketplace, 78% of all shoppers use the Internet to research and make purchase choices of products and services, according to the most recent report from Cisco Internet Business Solutions Group (IBSG)." Well, more than 60% of Internet information access and consumer research is done via mobile device.

Folks take their phones on their exercise runs to listen to music, listen to podcasts, listen to instructional information, motivational pieces, or exercise coaching, as well as mapping the distance and pace of their run/walk. They take photos with their phone. It's in the car when driving, possibly giving providing directions to their destination. Many people charge their phone near their bed as they sleep. Most smartphone owners are rarely more than three or four feet away from their cell phone, 24 hours a day/7 days a week/365 days a year.

I heard not too long ago about a product you can put your smartphone inside of so you can take your phone into the shower with you and access your music. I thought I was "tethered" to my phone but even I'm not **that** tethered.

What About Purely Local Business: Gardeners, Plumbers, Cleaners, Etc.?

What if your business is **strictly** local? If yours is a business that is obligated to only work locally, such as a cleaner, gardener, landscaper, or contractor, does any of this social media marketing make sense for you?

Maybe you already have a website because someone said you should. You've had this Website for four years, but you are thinking, "Why do I really do this? I'm not going to mow lawns or fix plumbing in Albuquerque or New Jersey. Why am I marketing online when my business only covers a very small area of my location in Southern California?"

People do shop online to find local business options. As mentioned earlier, there has been a greater increase every year of individuals who do Internet searching to find local businesses. Every year, increasingly high percentages of individuals search the Internet for what they want before they go out to purchase it. These increased percentages include a higher incidence of consumers researching on the Internet first to discover a local business solution rather than just-any-business-out-there. It's time more local businesses took advantage of this local-interest growth!

Customer Review Sites & Online Directories with a Local Search Function

Listing your business in local directories and larger-scope directories, with a local search function, such as Google and Bing, is an excellent way to also gain higher search engine ranking within a category. This happens when you include your location (neighborhood/city/county) in your marketing content and within any necessary, specified fields of directories with local search functions. If you don't already have one, get a free business listing in Google and Bing search engines. Utilize all free features available to you, keenly focusing on local search options.

Also list your business in the free-to-list online directories. For example, Merchant Circle, and customer review sites, such as Yelp, are also available to you. Utilize all of the free features each online directory offers. See if you can find any industry-specific directories that might also exist for your type of business, which also offer local search capabilities, such as Trip Advisor or Urban Spoon.

Facebook as a Social Media Marketing Channel

For those of you who don't already know, there are a number of ways to participate on Facebook: Personal Profile (yourself as an individual), Facebook Fan Page (as a business, a brand or celebrity/personality), Open Facebook Groups (anyone can join), Closed/Secret Facebook Groups (have to request permission to join from an Administrator of that Facebook Group) as well as a couple of other, less popular, uses.

Each individual must start with a Facebook Personal Profile. Meaning, before you can create a business page for your business (Fan Page, Open Facebook Group, Closed/Secret Facebook Group), you must first create a Facebook Personal Profile. No one needs to know who created your Facebook Fan Page or Group but they will be able to see who the administrator is. There needs to be at least one person administrating a Fan Page or Group. In the beginning, for smaller businesses at least, that is usually the person who created the Page/Group.

Facebook is an incredibly powerful social medium and can also be a powerful social media marketing tool. Only two years ago, reports on social media activity contained quotes that "1 out of 9 people on the planet had a Facebook profile." Now, per GlobalWebIndex.net Third Quarter 2013 Report, Facebook has fifty percent of the world's Internet users as **active** Facebook users. So, as a business owner, if you still believe that your customers aren't on Facebook, read that statement one more time—that is **huge!** And 75% of those Facebook users login at least once per day. When they say **active**, they aren't kidding. Add to that, there are multiple ways to utilize Facebook for social media marketing, even without paying for Facebook Ads.

Why Can't Facebook Be My Business Blog?

Before choosing Facebook as THE place to focus all of your social media marketing and target audience engagement, it is important to understand that Facebook is an **environment**—one controlled by someone other than you. As far as marketing goes, what you can do in Facebook now may not be what you can do six months from now. Basically, you don't want your only business blog to be Facebook because Facebook may change something that significantly impacts how you were utilizing it for your marketing.

For instance, Facebook could shut down your Facebook profile because they don't approve of the activity there, i.e. trying to friend too many people too quickly, conducting business too actively on your Facebook personal profile, etc. Yes, many people do actively use their Facebook profile as their business page. These individuals are operating on borrowed time. Now that Facebook is publically traded, those days could be numbered—not an effective way to conduct business. Facebook can, and has, shut down personal profiles, company pages, and business fan pages. If Facebook is your only social media marketing channel, you're giving away your power.

Recently, there has been the capability of pulling your blog into your Facebook Fan Page, a feature of Facebook which may, or may not, continue. For the time that this remains possible, Facebook does earn a broader exposure for your blog. But when your blog is viewed as a 'pull' into the Facebook environment, which one of you 'owns' the Web traffic to your blog? The answer: I don't know. I've asked several revered Facebook experts. Some of the responses were, "Oh, I didn't think about that," or "I have no idea," or "I'll try to find out and get back to you." None have ever come up with an answer for me. I've even asked Facebook—before and after they went public. I still don't have an answer from Facebook. That isn't to say they are avoiding my question specifically. Facebook is just known for not responding to questions directly.

What if Facebook gets credit for the traffic your blog pulls into Fan Pages since it's in their environment and not yours? If most of the traffic for your blog happens on your Facebook Fan Page, then your search engine rankings are taking a big hit. This is just something you should be aware of before deciding to take that action.

The Magic of Closed/Private Facebook Groups

Facebook Open Groups allow anyone to join. On the other hand, Facebook Closed Groups/Secret Groups require permission to join and are one of the greatest tools for creating ongoing engagement with your customers. For you, as a business owner, Closed/Secret groups are more powerful than open groups because of their exclusivity. Being part of an exclusive group, a sort of online country club, is far more enticing than being part of a group that "just anyone" can belong to. Closed/Secret Groups have several great benefits for you and your customers. For example, say you have a service business. You provide instructional seminars or live workshops on a particular topic.

During your seminar/workshop you invite those who paid to attend your seminar or live workshop to join a Closed/Secret Facebook Group, created exclusively for your seminar/workshop participants. You provide your participants with the Web address (URL) of your Facebook Closed/Secret Group.

You ask that once they have been added to the group, they create a post to introduce themself to the group. This post should include who they are, the nature their business, and what they wanted most to achieve from attending the seminar/workshop. Those who want to participate go to that URL and ask to join. You, or someone else administrating that group, verify their eligibility then accept their request to join the group.

This Facebook Closed/Secret Group serves as an online community/"country club," where your attendees who share a common interest in learning the topic of your seminar/workshop, can stay in touch with each other. This online community is an incredible channel for engaging with your customers while also providing a vehicle for your customers to engage with and learn from each other. There are several especially useful ways these groups can help you and your customers:

- Group/Community members get to bounce ideas off of each other. This "bouncing of ideas" off of several other individuals who are working toward a similar result, is called crowd-sourcing. Crowd-sourcing is a powerful and cost-effective vehicle for testing ideas, phrases, book titles, program titles, resources for needed services, identifying new services to establish, etc.

- Participants maintain a level of ongoing access to you and your information, which they have already proved they want.

- If you had exercises during your seminar/workshops, participants can continue to develop that work in the Closed/Secret Group.

- Some group members may even end up collaborating with other members, forming joint business ventures. I've seen this happen a number of times. As a business owner myself, I love these Closed/Secret Groups and am active in Closed/Secret Groups with each of my mentors who have them.

- It is a place for you to advise your participants/customers of new seminars, workshops, books, and articles you create which focus on information that is important to them. Such a community **IS** your target audience. They are already your customers. It is also a sounding board for what your audience needs—another source of marketing content. And here you can continue to serve these customers and provide opportunities for them to be repeat customers—in a manner that is beneficial for all of you!

You don't have to be a public speaker or instructor to utilize Facebook Closed/Secret Groups. Remember our BBQ grill stores from earlier in the book? If you owned one of the BBQ grill and patio businesses, you could create a Facebook Closed/Secret

Group for your customers to share with each other. Additionally, you could occasionally post BBQ recipes, grilling tips, or patio layout ideas to your group. You could also advise your group of store specials allowing them "extra hours of special pricing" by mentioning a 'secret word' the evening before, or the day before, the sale starts for the general public.

But I Don't Have Time To Keep Checking My Computer for Posts To My Social Media

Too busy to check your computer for notifications from your social media? "Gee, when was the last time somebody checked our Fan Page? Has somebody asked me a question and I'm not seeing it?" Have notifications from your Fan Page/Group sent to your cell phone by text or email. You can be notified by cell phone immediately, if someone posts a question on your Facebook Fan Page or Group Page; you can even see what that question is.

Even if you can't get to your computer, you would have the capability of responding right from your smartphone, if you have, or will consider getting, a smartphone that can handle email. If you are resistant to smartphones, this isn't going to happen for you. However, you should consider that a smartphone is a very powerful, time-saving tool for a small business owner always on the move and wanting to grow their business.

Can Creating YouTube Videos Make You A How-To Expert?

In Chapter One we talked about adding story to your marketing piece and part of why television is so 'addicting'; people love story and they love to "watch" story. Visual story-telling is highly desirable. For instance, I talked with you about River Pools and Spas who made lots of short how-it's-done videos about their business. These videos got lots of "views" (were watched by many different individuals.) River Pools and Spas took their FAQs and their SAQs (Should Ask Questions) to create these blog posts and videos.

Did you know that Google strips the dialogue out of YouTube videos so it sees it and evaluates that dialogue for keywords? If you have all kinds of keywords put around a blog posting and/or the description of a video, but what is said in that video doesn't match that description, Google knows and 'says', "Ha, nice try. Not ranking you." But when you are doing what you should be doing, making content in your video match descriptions and postings about the video—viola! Another boost to your search engine ranking!

This really is do-able for any small business. We are not talking about high-end video here. We are talking FlipCam/mini-cam type video. Video that you may well be able to do with just your smartphone, with you just you talking to your customers about what you do. You may feel that you don't look like a movie star, but your customers don't want a movie star. They want information from someone who knows what they are doing in their business, someone who understands their needs, problems and concerns. Your customers don't want feature films here; they want some valid information about a specific topic or concern. Your videos may only be from 2-8 minutes long, but it is long enough to pose a question and answer that question so that it is easy to understand.

Your video image does not need to be amazing. It does not need to be an example of fabulous lighting, it just needs to be understandable. The audio needs to be clear; this is more important than the quality of your video image. (A couple of mini-cam makers offer models with an external microphone jack, which further improves your audio.) The information also needs to be on-topic and helpful. That's all! You can do this. The more 'grass roots' your video appears, the more believable it is perceived to be by consumers.

Video marketing is such a powerful tool. Storing your business videos on YouTube and embedding them in blog posts on your Website, is also yet another boost for your search engine rankings.

Practice with this some. Before you say, "Never!" just try it. Try it six or seven times with a family member, a friend, your dog or the lamp in the living room. Just practice, several times, before you completely dismiss this option. You may surprise yourself.

Maybe you won't want start with video; it can be more time consuming than text or audio. However, it could be something to weave into your future social media marketing efforts. If you give video a try, you may discover that making short videos comes more easily to you than writing blog posts. If that is the case, do the videos and have someone transcribe the audio from your videos for the text portion of your blog!

Owning Your Own Marketing Channels Is Vital!

The social media platforms available for consumers and business owners are incredible 'sharing vehicles.' Facebook, YouTube, Pinterest, Twitter, etc. allow a level of communication and information sharing that boggles the mind! On a personal level, we can just experiment to discover which one, or ones, we like best and enjoy those social environments. However, as business owners, we are participating in social media for different reasons, with different objectives.

As business owners, we aren't simply participating in social media. We are participating in social media marketing. It is still about discovery; we must discover which platforms (Facebook, YouTube, etc.) are best suited for us to use, or to start with. We must also decide which social media types/channels (Blog, Email, Pinterest, Facebook Fan Page, Facebook Closed Group, etc.) within and across those platforms we are going to use, or start with.

However, as business owners, we need to keep the future in mind. We must take into consideration access to, and retrieve-ability of, our online content six months from now, six years from now, and so on. I mentioned that it is not wise to plan with your only business blog being a Facebook Fan Page or Facebook Group, as Facebook may change something that significantly impacts your marketing. The same applies to any other social media environment.

It is vital that your business have online marketing channels where your content is owned by you and controlled by you! Content that won't disappear because Facebook blows up one day or goes off the market completely. Your business' intellectual property—your informational content—needs to be under your control, or you risk losing months or years of your online blog articles/posts because something happens with Facebook, LinkedIN, or a free blogging site that you chose to use for your business blog.

Facebook, YouTube, LinkedIN, Twitter—these are all online 'environments.' These environments are created and controlled by someone other than you. They are great and powerful environments, but not under your control, so they are not the best choice to be the "core" of your online marketing.

Which Channels Should be The Core of Your Social Media Marketing?

There are two channels vital to your social media marketing. They are the two you can own and control:

1. your blog, when that blog is in a domain which you own, and
2. your email list(s) and the content you create in your email marketing.

THE most powerful choice for your business is to have these two channels as the core of your social media marketing. When you are choosing which types of social media to utilize in your business, if you can only start with two—these are the two to start with. You can add another channel, or two, or three, once you have worked these two into your regular business operations.

What IS A Blog?

You may be asking yourself, "How can I start a blog and use it as a marketing tool when I don't know what a blog is?" Well, you're not alone. Many people don't really know what a blog is. 'Blog' is one of those terms that people hear, and may even use, over and over without really knowing what it means.

There are many business owners who believe they should have a blog even though they aren't certain what a blog is. However, it's difficult to strategize for something you don't understand, so here's a super simple definition of a blog: a blog is, essentially, an online journal. Not a personal diary—that record which, if your brother or sister found and read it, would make you want to crawl in a hole and disappear.

We are talking global platform here. You WANT lots of people to read it. A blog is a journal of the author's experiences, observations, and opinions; it may even contain photos, audio files and videos—definitely not your classic diary! Blogs actually used to be called "Web logs." Around the year 2000, "We**blog**" began taking on a popular nickname—"blog." Congratulations! You are now among the small percentage of people who could actually define the word blog.

Your Blog: Your Most Powerful Marketing Tool

This blog, a virtual journal, could be something that's very personal to you. You could share personal insights with other people, or you could make this an amazing business tool. For instance, your blog can be a place where you post frequently asked questions (FAQs). As mentioned above, blogs can also contain photos, audio files and videos, providing a one-stop shop filled with all types of media for your target audience to choose from. Whoo-hoo!

Your target audience can also comment on your blog posts. In your blog, or blogs, you have the option of allowing or not allowing your blog readers this ability. Either way, each of your FAQs can exist as a text blog post, an audio file (which might also be a podcast show), and a video. Many of these comments could turn into yet more content that should be addressed in your blog or other marketing message content. Allowing your target audience to comment enhances engagement with your target audience. You will learn from what your target audience is looking for as much as, if not more than, they learn from what you "post" there. Remember, your target audience is a valuable source of content!

As for domains, your blog can be a WordPress blog but not on WordPress's Website. Your business blog needs to be in a domain under your control.

I would suggest a blog option that allows for photos, audio and video. That is not to say you need to start with all of that. You may well want to start with only text. However, if your blog template allows for all media, it provides room for future growth for your business.

Do you remember when we talked about being your own SEO (Search Engine Optimization) Strategist? Let me refresh your memory, just in case. When your marketing messages and Website content are focused on serving your customers and your potential customers (your target audience), and there is thoughtful consideration of which keywords your customers and target audience would most likely be using, your Website content IS your SEO strategy. All with**out** paying for AdWords and expensive SEO consultations!

Why Are Blogs So Great For Search Engine Optimization (SEO)?

Are you feeling a bit like having a blog for your business doesn't sound like REAL social media? You may be more interested in getting involved in some real social media by marketing on Facebook, YouTube, or another of the social media environments, before spending time on something as mundane as a blog. After all, the other things are cooler, more business-sexy than just having a blog.

Let me help you see a blog as a cool, business-sexy social media marketing hero! First, we need to chat about search engines and search engine optimization (SEO). You know you want high rankings in search engines so your target audience can find you and visit your Website. They like what they find and want more of your information. They come to respect and trust you and, optimally, become repeat customers and raving fans of your business.

In the first two chapters we talked about how best to develop your marketing messages to see that this happens. A very important part of this process involves Internet search engines. So, these search engines that you want so desperately to optimize your business presence in—what do they really do?

The core of what search engines do is 'search' for frequent, relative content. You type into the search box of a search engine what it is that you want to look for. The search engine considers the words/terms you typed into the box as "keywords" and looks through what is available to it on the Internet. It returns a— usually staggeringly long—list of "search results." Those search results were chosen as being "relevant" to your search inquiry. Search results are listed with the most relevant results first, then on down the long, long list of results to the least relevant.

So, why do search engines LOVE blogs? Blogs are created around specific topics or areas of interest. And when blog authors post frequently on specific areas of interest, blogs become the search engine's Holy Grail of frequent, relevant content! The more frequent and relevant the content of your business blog, the more of a boost to your search engine results—on an ongoing basis!

Now can you appreciate why having a blog with a text portion, a video portion and an audio portion--three media versions of one specific concern—is a good thing for your business? These mean better search engine results for your business as well as more multi-media options for your target audience! Good stuff! Here's another, even edgier way to look at it. Blogs are more than candy for search engines; blogs are like crack cocaine for search engines. Search engines can't help but love them; it's central to their programming! Blogs increase your search engine optimization by their very nature. Huzzah! How's that for cool social media and business-sexy marketing?

One more point: be aware that Facebook, Twitter, LinkedIN, and online customer review sites are all considered mini-blogs in the world of search engines. And remember, search engines love blogs, even mini-blogs! That's just something to think about when you are formulating your decisions about your social media marketing choices.

Your Email List And Email Marketing

Your thoughts on email marketing and the list you develop to increase your marketing reach may seem un-exciting and a bit like "old tech." However, there are numerous great ways to conscientiously grow email lists and use those lists to serve your prospects and customers as well as powerfully benefit your business. Email marketing is also something you own and control, so it will not simply go away someday as "Likes" for your Facebook Fan Page could. If changes occur in any social media environment and negatively impact your established marketing strategies, you need to have core strategies in place which you own and control. These core channels will keep you "virtually afloat" as you establish any new social media marketing channels you can pursue. Additionally, for the percentage of your target audience who are not yet especially active in social media environments, email is your best option for staying in touch, engaging, and serving those individuals.

Earlier, we were talking about being notified of social media posts. You don't have to wonder whether there might be a relevant email that you should be responding to. If you have, or are willing to consider getting, a smartphone that can handle email. Simply have your Website inquiry/email marketing Inbox set up in your smartphone. If you are resistant to smartphones, this isn't going to happen for you. But once again, a smartphone is a very powerful tool for a small business owner strapped for time.

Podcasting—The Under-utilized Gold Mine Of Marketing

Podcasting is also a channel you can own, as long as you

maintain a back-up archive of your podcast episodes. Generally, you have a podcast hosted in another environment to avoid problems of the audio not playing properly due to any technical issues on your Website. If, several years down the road, something happens to the environment where you currently store your podcast, you will still have your content to establish it in a new environment, provided you have maintained your own back-up of all of your podcast episodes.

But What About My Traditional Marketing, You Ask?

What if you are a business owner who has been marketing for years, with an established marketing plan composed of predominately traditional marketing: Yellow Pages, print, radio spots, direct mail, neighborhood papers, Val-Paks, et cetera and possibly a Website? What if you think, "I can't afford to add anything to my marketing budget. And why should I stop doing any of the marketing I've been doing for years?"

Even though you may have your online Yellow Page piece, the expense for the print aspect of a Yellow Pages listing, or ad, is quite high. General statistics also show year over year declining returns. You may need to test-drive a new marketing channel and see some results from it before you are willing to commit additional marketing funds or re-direct a significant percentage of your funds away from any one of your traditional marketing channels, but I assure you it can be worth it.

There's no denying that business owners with carefully structured marketing strategies which they have continued using for years, can become attached to those strategies—even if those strategies aren't providing effective returns on their investment. Furthermore, not all business owners will know, if asked, "How much is it, exactly, that you are spending on your individual marketing channels per month/quarter?" Business owners frequently know the collective amount, but may or may not be able to quote individual costs without reviewing invoices or accounting information.

How to Give Social Media Marketing a Chance in Your Business, With an Already Fixed Budget

One way to test-drive social media channels for inclusion into your overall marketing strategy: take a look at your accounting information and see which of your traditional marketing channels might have a percentage of flux. Which one thing would you be willing to change? What percentage of your collective marketing budget would you be willing to re-direct to a new social media marketing channel. Depending on the size of your marketing budget, say 5%, 10%, 15%, 20%?

Which social media channel will it be? For one business, the choice may be blogging. For another, it may be Pinterest. It might be a podcast or a Facebook Fan Page. The choice depends on what matters most to your business.

Take one social media channel and commit to it for nine to twelve months. Track the new channel for increases in traffic, leads, conversions and sales. Then measure from that change.

In your traditional marketing, direct marketing can be tracked but results from print Yellow Pages listings and ads can be tougher to identify. As can radio and television spots. It's a tough sell for some business owners to accept, but while you may be very attached to your traditional marketing the potential market gain from effective social media marketing strategies, also known as inbound marketing, is a necessary shift that you can't afford to ignore for much longer.

I am not suggesting that you systematically eliminate all of your traditional marketing channels. Just that you systematically shift funds from lesser-performing marketing channels to potentially higher-performing social media channels. When you start seeing the comparison costs vs. returns on investments compared to traditional marketing costs, you can make a more informed choice about a new, more comprehensive and higher performing overall marketing strategy.

6

How to Almost Painlessly Incorporate A Social Media Marketing Campaign Into Your Regular Business Operations and Not Just as Something Else To Be Done

This is where you bring together your learning from the previous chapters and weave your new operational requirements into your regular business operations. Yes, there is a learning curve for anything new we undertake. However, in this chapter, you will find tips for managing these new operational requirements. With some creative considerations and planning, weaving the operational requirements of your new social media marketing channel(s) into your regular business operations can be, almost, painless.

Digging for Your Content Treasures, Step-by-Step

Part of what is going to make this almost painless is not having to "start from scratch" with figuring out where to find content for your new social media marketing channels.

You already know where to find that content. We discussed this in Chapter 4, "Where to Find Untapped Treasures for Your Social Media Content That Already Exist in Your Business." It is anywhere information queries were written: in an e-mail, in a memo, in any kind of notation that occurs within your business. Also, consider looking through purchase orders or invoice problems for ideas. If you have been allowing customers/prospects questions to 'die' until now, start documenting inquiries from customers/prospects immediately. These are content treasures! Any source of inbound questions/concerns from customers and prospects, that isn't already recorded per your company policy would be an item for your Marketing To Do List. So:

1. In case you didn't take any notes about where these untapped treasures might be found in your business, review Chapter 4 and make a list of places you can find your content.

2. Once you have your list, decide on a span of time to review. For this first dip into your untapped treasures of content, try a time span of somewhere between 30-120 days. If yours is a very small business, you may need the longer period of time to find a collection of content to begin with. A somewhat larger business may only need to review the last 30 days of emails, customer calls, memos, etc. to find a collection of content to begin with.

3. Be systematic about going through your untapped treasures. Create a file (paper or digital) of the items you discover. Make copies (paper or digital) of the 'content treasures' you find.

4. Begin your search reviewing from yesterday (the day before you began your search) and work backward in

time. Make a note of where you left off at the end of each 'span of time' for your review sessions. This method is particularly helpful if you are doing your reviews in bits of free time each day, since you will always know where you left-off during your last search.

5. As you go through this initial treasure hunt for content, you will find that other ideas for content as well as thoughts for other places to look for existing content, will come to you. Write those ideas down on paper or type them into a computer file titled "Content Treasures and Ideas—Your Name." Put your "Ideas" category at the top of the page/file as there will be fewer of those than the items for content you will find during your reviews.

6. Once the review of untapped treasures for a given time span has been completed, create a description, synopsis or Q&A for each content item. If a particular question or concern came up multiple times, write "occurrences" somewhere near your description and tally the number of occurrences with hash marks. Items with multiple occurrences demonstrate that more people want to know about that item/question/concern; those should be addressed first.

7. Whether you have one person review all of your untapped treasures or you divide the responsibilities, once the list of content items, with descriptions, is complete, it's time for a business meeting. See the subheading, 'Your Treasure Council' for details about this meeting agenda.

HOT TIP

As you go through this initial treasure hunt for content, other ideas will come to you. Write those ideas down on paper or type them into a computer file. Be systematic about going through your untapped treasures. Make a copy of the information (paper or digital) and create a file (paper or digital) of the items you discover. This method is particularly helpful if you are doing your reviews in bits of time each day.

One business I know of found over 260 content pieces they could use after going through their untapped treasures. Before digging for their untapped treasures, they had no idea that they were in possession of all this content. Even if they were posting to their new blog every day, that content would spread over nearly two-thirds of a year. If they posted every week, it would last almost five years! They have enough content for a very long time. At this point, it's just a matter of typing it out and developing it into a customer-focused post or article, then placing it into your social media production schedule.

More Hidden Content Treasure

It is also important to realize that you are "cursed" with your knowledge of the details in your business. Other people simply don't know all that you know about what you do in your business or how your products/services come to exist. If this sounds too cryptic, consider the concept this way: in contrast to those questions customers and prospects frequently ask you about your business, **you** know which questions they should be asking but don't. This is because they just don't know enough about your business to ask.

As humans, we often assume that others know what we know about things we are familiar with. We think, "Oh, they know that." No, a lot of people don't know what you know about your business: how you make/develop your products for them, how you develop your services for them—these are all mysteries, so tell them! Better yet, show your customers how you do what you do, in a video. This is content! Use it!

Your content is there. It has simply been waiting to be recognized. Now, it is only a matter of pulling your content out of hiding and 'dressing it up' for publication. How much content treasure will you find in your business?

Your First 'Treasure Council' Meeting Agenda

Armed with the results of your first untapped treasures review, you call a business meeting. Your agenda:

1. Decide, in order of best results which untapped treasure sources proved most fruitful. This is for future occasions, when time is the tightest and you have to choose where to focus your energies. You might conduct reviews every 2-3 months, until you have reviewed all of your historical data, depending on how much content you need. Or you may choose to go through all of your treasures at once. That choice depends on the time you have, the length of time you've been in business and the size of your business.

2. Determine which topics/concerns discovered you will use as content and in what order.

3. If, initially, you are only providing one media form, e.g. text for a blog article, then you won't need to decide how many forms of media to create for each topic/concern. If you are using more than one form of media, say text and audio, and/or video, you will also want to decide which and how many forms of media you will create for each piece of content

4. Determine where you will place each media form for each piece of content:
   a. Text—on your blog, your Facebook Fan Page, Group, Twitter and/or LinkedIN, post an update to your social media channels that is appropriate for that piece of content. This is "search engine candy"
   b. Podcast—post the audio on your blog as well as in iTunes. If you have a Facebook Fan Page, Group, Twitter and/or LinkedIN, post an update to each channel that is appropriate for that piece of content. Again, this is "search engine candy."
   c. Video—place your videos on YouTube and embed them in your blog post; more "search engine candy."

5. Decide on a minimum and maximum posting frequency for placing content in your social media.

6. Besides this schedule for marketing content, figure out how you will be responding to comments and postings that come from your social media channels. You will likely respond to comments and postings from customers/prospects as they happen, but you also might schedule "social media rounds" three times a day. Five minutes at the start of the business day, mid-day and near closing can be used to determine if a response is needed for responding to a posting.

7. Decide how often to conduct treasure hunts for content and what span of time to cover each time, until you've gone through your historical data. Keep in mind:

    a. Once the review of your historical data has been completed, then you can work forward from the date of your first treasure hunt review.

    b. By this time, you will have created a system that works for your business to identify content pieces as they come in, and you can simply work those into your content creation schedule.

    c. Of course, there will always be customer inquiries which need to be addressed immediately. Review Chapter 4, subheading "Hidden content treasures waiting to be found by you." for how to make the most of customer/prospect inquiries.

8. Identify who, or who-all, will be:

    a. conducting your future content treasure hunts,

    b. creating the posts for your social media, and

    c. conducting your 'social media rounds.

Deciding on a Frequency for Publishing Your Social Media Content

Quality content which addresses the concerns of your target audience is far more valuable to that target audience and your bottom line than simply pumping out postings which have no real value to anyone. The absolute minimum for publishing new marketing content should be one per month. Once every two weeks is a better pattern choice. You could also plan on one per week. I wouldn't suggest planning for more than once per week, though. No one really wants to hear from your business more often than once per week. My personal favorite is once every two weeks.

Remember to take into consideration that you are in the process of re-developing how you write your marketing messages, making them 'customer-focused.' This critical component to getting game-changing results for your new social media marketing strategy, means you might want to start with posting once a month while you develop your skills at writing customer-focused content. Then, decide if you want to produce marketing content more often than once a month. If you are creating more than one type of media (text, audio, video) for each piece of content, you are going to attract a good deal of attention for each one. Work smarter, not harder!

Will You Give Up The Power of "Your Business Voice"?

Who will be your business voice? This choice is a "biggie"! We 'flashback' to Chapter 3 where we talked about giving away vs. taking control of your "business voice." Are you going to outsource your social media posting? Turn over your "business voice" to someone who doesn't really understand your business, or the language of your business, the culture of our business? Shouldn't the voice of your business understand what lives in you, as a business owner?

Get Your Own People Involved in "Your Business Voice"!

Rather than give up this perfect tool, are you going to have your business voice come from within your business? Your business voice doesn't have to be you, the owner. Granted, yours would be the most passionate voice, but people within your business do understand your business. Okay, there might an exception or two. There are always those who just clock in, do their thing and go home. However, for the most part, people within your business understand your business and want it to do well; your business is also their livelihood.

So, get your people involved in your new marketing plan. When you have your own employees working in your social media marketing channels, your social media content will have more vibrance; more life, and more dimension.

To gear your new marketing toward success, assign someone who you believe has good communication skills. The "how" of doing social media is much easier to learn than learning how to communicate with and relate to people. Don't assign your social media postings to "Bob," if Bob would rather have a root canal than do this type of work. Yet even Bob knows more about your business than a marketer., so look for someone in your business who is suited to the task. There are always people who thrive on doing this kind of work and they will usually be happy to help. That person could be thinking, "Wow! You want to hear what I have to say about our business? I could be talking to our customers by authoring our business blog!?"

You may even have employees who would be totally excited about this new work. You may have an employee who has been looking for a way to have a voice in your business. It might be your customer service person, that individual who gets those "figurative" 50 millimeter ammunition shells shot across their ears all day, every day. It could also be the person who hears all the horror stories of customer complaints. This could be their opportunity to **create something** instead of just "dodging bullets" all day. Bottom line, you just might be surprised when you hold your Treasure Council meeting and start brainstorming about who will be doing which social media marketing tasks.

If you don't have someone who is especially excited to author your social media, you might divide and/or rotate the responsibilities. When the responsibilities are being shared, no one person has to do so much and, together, everyone can achieve massive awesomeness. One option for dividing the responsibilities is to have one person review your untapped treasure sources, another writes and posts the content and yet another does your 'social media rounds' each day. Or, you might divide the responsibilities between two, or three, individuals and rotate the duties every two to four weeks. This allows enough time to get comfortable with a schedule of tasks, but also enough "change up" to keep tasks from becoming too routine.

Depending on your business situation, it might prove best to have more than one individual providing your business voice. Two or three perspectives speaking, instead of "All things according to Employee X," might be what works best in your business. It's up to you—you know your business best.

A Plan for the One-Woman/One-Man Business

For the solo entrepreneur thinking, "How do I fit this in when I barely have time to get all my other business things happening? I don't have any employees or partners, I am the one and only person in this business. How am I going to make time for this?" Yes, your situation is not the same as for a business with employees. However, earlier we talked about the importance of getting some social media marketing going for your business because it is no longer a luxury, it has become a necessity.

That said, how do you handle incorporating additional tasks when you're absolutely the only person for the task, for any task. Already, you barely have time to pee or eat, let alone take on more tasks. That **is** a tough challenge. Where do you "find" time? The way to "find" time does take some practice. I wish I could just touch you with a wand and create the time for you but I can't. The truth is, we all get the same amount of time. We have to choose where we spend—invest—the time given. BUT the time you spend to "find time," is time **invested**, and social media is a more than sound investment.

An Exercise for "Finding" The Time You Need for Social Media

Time is invested in your business and for your business. Over the period of a week, document the time you spend doing what you do—at work and at home. Why so many days? There are a couple of reasons for this: 1) you aren't accustomed to doing this and you will notice some activities on one day that you miss on another day. You can correct for these as you notice them over the course of this week. 2) there may well be certain tasks that only come up on certain days.

Why am I asking that you also track you time at home? As a business owner, you may well be doing a fair amount of work at home. That time spent needs to be identified as well. Besides, while we are in search of time, wouldn't it be great to increase some of our at home time—reducing, or removing, business work done at home.

How are you supposed to record this? If you prefer paper, order a spiral bound appointment book like hairstylists, Chiropractors, etc., use. This is the kind that are broken down into 10 or 15 min intervals. I would avoid trying to use a wallet-size appt. book., since your notes would be too tiny or each day take up too many pages to effectively complete this recording process. This tiny size would not provide the visual realization that a larger format will provide when you review your days. Go for a full-size 8 ½" x 11" (some may have slightly larger dimensions) and simply carry it around with you, open to the current day, then make brackets covering the time span of each activity with a note on what you were doing.

After doing this for two days, it will become easier. By the end of the third day, you will start becoming aware of some patterns. You will also notice some "time holes" in your days. Some of those "time holes" may be something you missed recording and you can fill those spaces in. However, you will also see "holes" that are really pieces of time where you weren't doing anything. You may have "felt" busy at that time but you weren't really accomplishing a particular task. This will probably produce some mixed feelings: some surprise, some disbelief, maybe even some upset—that there has been some available time which going unused as well as unnoticed.

At the end of a week of recording your activities, set aside—invest—a good two to four hours time, at home if necessary, to really look at this documentation. First look for those "holes" of time. Make a note of how much time that adds up to during each of your business days that you tracked. Take note of the different activities/tasks you did each day. List them. How much time did you spend on a given task each day? How many tasks did you do each day. Now look through your records of your time at home. How much time did you spend working on business at home during that week? Was there time spent on business work at home every day? How much time each day?

What did you find? How many "holes" of time did you find? How much time did those "holes" add up to: over the course of each day? Over the week? There are five things you can do with all of this information:

1. Discover time that is wasted. If we really look at how we move through our business activities each day, usually, we can identify bits of time-waste here and there. Time that can be put to more productive use.

2. Identify any duplication or unwarranted repetition of operational tasks.

3. Armed with the results of 1 and 2 above, spend 20-60 minutes each day to chart your next day of business activity. Do this either at the end of your business day or at home before going to bed, whichever provides the appropriate clear, uninterrupted time. Schedule your day; your regular tasks and assign those "holes" of wasted time to the development your social media marketing program. Even if it's only 15 minutes each

day or 40 minutes each week—START! Start treasure hunting for your content, then 'dressing up' your content and posting it to your blog. Remember, if you can have only one piece of social media marketing, make it a blog!

4. Go to MIYPmarketing.com/SBBP, or search iTunes, for "The Small Businesses Solving BIG Problems Show with Viver Israel" to hear interviews with other small business owners and what has worked, or not worked, for them in getting everything done in their business. You will also hear how they work through other business challenges, their best and worse marketing efforts, biggest business regret and best business tip. New episodes are published the first and third Tuesday of each month. "Show Notes" for each episode are also available at the MIYPmarketing.com Website, under the "Blogs" menu.

5. During your week of documenting time, you also identified how much of your "at-home" time is being taken away by business duties. Once you have developed your social media marketing strategy and some skills at re-focusing your marketing messages to be more customer-focused, you will be able to, again, free-up some "holes" of time. Some of those "holes," dedicated to making time for your new marketing program; can now be used to free up your "at home" time. Having more "off-duty" time will improve your off-work life and help you perform better while at your business.

Do Your Marketing Videos Need to be Fancy & Polished?

No. An informal video can absolutely be taken by a flip cam and feature an ordinary person sitting at a table, or counter, speaking off the cuff about a topic they are passionate about. Honestly, the non-uber-polished videos really bring better results. There is a higher level of trust for informal videos than for highly-polished corporate-like videos.

There is such a difference in the depth of bonding that happens with a video as the customer/prospect is watching you speak to them. When you're looking at someone in a video, you now have a sense of **knowing** that person. A similar occurrence happens in podcasting when customers/prospects hear your voice; they hear the passion. People want the information they are looking for, but they will be more attracted to sources of information that come from someone they perceive to be knowledgeable, passionate, and believable.

What If I Don't Have the Right Look for Video? What If I'm Not a Great Speaker?

Video marketing is great for relationship and trust-building. After all, video is one of the most powerful media available. Like podcasting, it is also extremely under-utilized. Often people are afraid to do video. They may feel, "I don't have the face for this. I'm not a good speaker." The truth is, you don't need to have "the face for it." You don't need to be a strong speaker. What you need is to know what it is you do and to be authentic. That's what your target audience is looking for; that's what matters to them.

How Long is a "Short Video"?

There are many recommendations for the length of a short, informational video. Depending on the source, the answers range from two to three minutes; maybe five, maybe even seven can also be an option. For instructional videos, recommendations are anywhere from 30 to 60 minutes. These recommendations are a bit like the "Pirate Code" from Disney's *Pirates of the Caribbean*. They're actually more like "guidelines." If you try to cram an answer to a question into a too-short video, your speech will be too fast and flustered, making it difficult for people to understand you.

Cutting out too much of your video content to meet a 2 or 3 minute 'time limit,' often leaves your video lacking effective coverage of the question/concern. Rushing does not serve your target audience.

Determining The Right Length for Your Videos

Does the content in your video, whatever the length, serve your target audience? Is it answering the question it poses? If you can say yes, then however long that video is, it is the length it needs to be. However, if your video is answering the question as though it were a James Michener novel, beginning with, "Once There Was a Dinosaur," and only e-ven-tu-al-ly getting around to your point—then your video is way too long and no one will watch it. Cut down the time!

If your video content is valuable to your target audience, they will watch it. If your target audience needs that information, it won't matter if the video is eight minutes long instead of two or three. If they need the answer to that question, if they need to know how to do something, such as get their toilet to stop spewing all over the bathroom, believe me, they'll sit and watch it. They'll watch it even if it's 12 minutes because that's a lot faster than the time it takes to get a plumber out to their home.

So, how long is a short video? It depends. The best rule of thumb is:

- Is the content valid and totally relevant to the particular question/concern it's discussing?

- Does the content in the video serve to answer the question from the customer's point of view and what matters to them?

- Does the content have a story aspect to it? Because that's truly what your target audience is going to remember.

- However long is required to succinctly satisfy the above criteria—that is the right length for your video.

What About Podcasting?

While there are podcasts with both audio and video, podcasts are predominately thought of as audio. You could call any audio file a podcast as long as it's somewhere on the Internet where people can connect to it and/or download it. If you made an audio file and just stored it on you computer where no one could access it, strictly speaking, you couldn't call it a podcast. These days, though, people refer to almost any audio file with information in it as a podcast. While that's not exactly accurate, the accuracy doesn't really matter. If your target audience sees something as a podcast, it's a podcast.

Podcasting is another under-utilized social marketing medium. As I mentioned earlier, when we talked about video, there is a very different bond created with podcasting. Your audience hears your energy and your personality in your voice. They can hear your passion for your topic. Podcasting is a such a great medium, and being under-utilized, it can provide an excellent conduit for bringing business to you. For many people, podcasting is easier to manage than videos. For the best exposure, get your podcast on iTunes where most people who are looking for podcasts do their podcast shopping!

Which Channels of Social Media Marketing Will You Start With?

Now that you have a sense of the different platforms and channels for social media marketing (Chapters 2 and 5), which will you choose for your business? Are there some social media tactics that are more powerful than others? The true answer to that is: it depends. It depends on what type of business you have, and what you, as the business owner, might be most comfortable with.

I'm going to assume that you aren't going to begin your venture into social media marketing with a full, across the board, social media marketing campaign. Even if you want a fully interlaced social media marketing strategy, it is more powerful to start with one to three channels. Become comfortable with weaving these channels into your regular business operations, and work effectively with those channels, before adding more.

If you want to know what I would recommend as the most

important thing for you to do in social media marketing, that would pretty much come back to "it depends." Basically, I would say a blog, a text blog. But if the business loves the idea of video then, by all means, they should start with video—a video blog.

If your business can start with only one social media marketing channel, the choice should be among the most powerful (blog, email, video, podcast). First, you should consider what is most comfortable for your business, and for you as a business owner. If you are undecided and can only do one thing, then hands down, make that one thing a blog. Blogs are a core media. They provide the most business traction and have the best all-around benefits. So, a blog is one of **the** best choices as the foundation of your social media marketing strategy. A blog in a domain you own is also one of the few marketing channels you can own and control.

Second, you can start an email marketing campaign or re-tool an existing program to be more customer-focused. Email is another of the marketing channels that you can own and control.

Third, either a podcast or videos. Both are very powerful and both are under-utilized. So, if your business utilizes these channels there are additional search engine optimization benefits for your business. Also, the variety of media will benefit your target audience.

Fourth, or third if you can't align yourself with either podcasting or videos, have a Facebook Closed/Secret Group for paying customers.

One very important reminder: the only thing worse than not having a social media marketing strategy is creating social media marketing channels, then abandoning them. If a social media presence is supposed to be your business and that presence is a ghost town, what does that say about how you do business? What does that say about how you follow up, and about how you treat your customers?

Reviewing The Process You've Learned

It isn't possible for me to put a full data download of what I know to do, here in a book. What I have put here will:

- Walk you through a process which you can use as a game-changer via re-developing your marketing messages as you develop **your** "Secret Sauce."

- Walk you through developing a Marketing To Do List specifically for your business

- Prove to you how powerfully an effective interlaced social media marketing program can empower your business growth.

- Give you a sense of the more powerful choices available in social media.

- Provide some ideas on how to use various social media marketing channels in your business.

- Guide you in how to discover untapped treasures of content for your social media postings, which already exist in your business.
    - All you need to do is 'un-earth' them and dress them up for publishing.

- Impress you with the importance of retaining control of your business voice.

- Finally, give you a step-by-step process for weaving your new content treasure hunt and social media marketing tasks into your regular business operations.

What To Do Next Checklist—Step-by-Step

- Prioritize your Marketing To Do List, from the items you added to this list as you read the book.

- Foundational to your Marketing To Do List should be re-developing your marketing messages to be customer-focused and include "story"—your "Secret Sauce."

- Seriously consider doing the Finding Time Exercise. That investment of time will free up time for you from this point forward.

- Use your notes to discover where your untapped treasures of content are likely to be found.

- Use the FREE Word of MOUSE Companion Workbook available for download at WordOfMouseBlog.com/workbook for checklists and writing action plans for your new marketing strategy.

- Review the HOT TIPS throughout the book.

- Start Step-by-Step Digging for your Content Treasures (in this Chapter).

- Hold your first 'Treasure Council' meeting and complete the agenda.

- Choose which social media marketing channels you will start your campaign with.

You can work through this list on your own, if you prefer. There is an enormous amount of information available on the Internet, and many instructional videos on YouTube, which may help you fill in some blanks as you work through building your new marketing strategy. Many people may choose this route. This method certainly **seems** more economical to a small business.

It seems to cost you less, in money, but it will cost you time. Possibly, too much time. When it comes to incorporating important processes into your business, you are not simply choosing one learning curve over another. You are also choosing a "results curve." If you don't stay on-task and on-target with exercising your new knowledge, re-developing your marketing messages ,and getting an effective social media marketing strategy in place, you will face a significant cost in wasted time. This also results in future, unrealized sales the longer you delay. Furthermore, if your strategy is not in its best form as it really should be to get the desired results, then you haven't chosen favorably by your business and you've cost yourself both time and money.

Whatever your choice, you have both the most to gain and the most to lose. Make a commitment to yourself to do this for your business. Give yourself a Date-to-Complete. Make the completion date realistic, but one that requires focused effort. You want to get this party started. You want to see results! If you slip in your commitment, re-commit. This is your livelihood we are talking about.

Utilize the step-by-step processes in the book. Utilize the checklists, worksheets and custom lists you build in the Word of MOUSE Companion Workbook.

If You Get Stuck, Call Me!

Doing this work on your own will take longer. That means more time before you start seeing results. If you get stuck, if you aren't sure how to change the focus of your marketing, aren't sure you're incorporating story into your message, aren't sure about how to put together an interlaced strategy or which channels would be most appropriate, that's when having an effective social media marketing consultant makes a difference. If you get stuck, consider engaging a social media marketing consultant—you can call me!

You may be thinking, "Well, of course, she's going to say call her." The truth is, an experienced professional can help make the learning curve a lot steeper. You'll get to results faster with the help of somebody familiar with the skills required. This is what I do when I am taking on a new skill or facet of business. I identify a mentor to learn from, then start working with that mentor so I can get the results I want with the least waste of time. I've come to learn such action actually cost me less.

Another thing that I like about hiring a skilled professional for new, or better, skills, is that they also provide structure and accountability. There's usually "homework" involved. They are providing me additional, structured direction so I can have the shortest path to success.

What Do I Do As A Social Media Marketing Consultant?

When you create your marketing pieces, and this is part of what I do, take what I have found is really working for businesses:

- review information about a 'client-business',
- learn something of that business' culture,
- learn what that business does and does not do in marketing,
- discover what 1-3 of their comparable competition businesses are and are not doing in marketing,
- work through the marketing message process we discuss in this book,
- identify any probable 'fast-start'-to-result marketing opportunities,
- coach the business in learning to identify 'hidden treasures' of marketing content already in their business,
- with knowledge of client-business culture, identify a best strategic 'start plan' and growth plan for social media and mobile marketing strategy plus the addition or shift of marketing dollars,
- integrate their new marketing plans and editorial schedule into their regular business operations, without it being just another thing that has to be dealt with,
- coach business on why to never turn over their 'business voice' to a marketer, and
- "graduate" business to emerge from their coaching, in control of their "business voice," effectively connected to and managing their own marketing as well as managing their target audience's response to that

content.

The difference with beginning with an effective social media marketing consultant is the coaching on which steps to take and when to take them. Someone who's going to help you build a good foundation, an infrastructure and a strategy to work from, can groom you for success. It's important that the pieces of your marketing come together well to perform most effectively, and with the shortest reasonable turnaround time. Then your marketing efforts start "snowballing," creating their own growth factor that can take you way beyond what you thought could happen with your marketing.

Apply for a FREE Consultation

Complete the form at MIYPmarketing.com/offer to apply for a FREE customer-focused social media marketing consultation.

If you want to take on doing this on your own, then go out there and more power to you. The very bottom line is START NOW! You might trip, you might fall but get started and keep going. If you find that the doing-it-on-your-own plan is not working for you or is not coming together fast enough for your needs, come on back. Contact me and let's work out the problems. We can get you to the level where your business needs to be.

Viver Winters Israel

About The Author

Vivianne "Viver" Israel is a Southern California native and mother of one, amazing, daughter. Raising her daughter on her own, Viver held multiple jobs, mainly as a Registered Nurse, to make those 'financial ends' more-than-just "meet."

Going on to become a serial entrepreneur, among her business endeavors, Viver founded a successful Internet Marketing business in 1996, when the commercial portion of the Internet was in its infancy. She also published two books on Internet Marketing: "How to Sell Your Books Online: A Step-by-Step Guide" and "Search Engines 101: A Website Owner's Guide to Understanding Search Engine Optimization."

When long-distance management of her mother's declining health became too much, Viver made the difficult decision to refer her clients out to her competition and closed her business.

Several years later, in 2008, rising victorious from her bout with metastatic breast cancer, Viver began studying the new technologies of Internet Marketing that were available and how they were, and were not, being utilized.

Starting a new Internet Marketing business in 2011, she focused on Social Media and Mobile Device Marketing. Using her own business as a lab to develop a powerful "Before and After" scenario, Viver spent the first 24 months "doing Internet Marketing" in the manner she saw many businesses utilizing . . . UN-successfully. Meanwhile, she searched for powerful examples of successful Social Media Marketing that resulted in real business growth!

Viver understands why many of the small businesses, and even large and enterprise-level businesses, utilizing Social Media aren't seeing effective 'take-it-to-the-bank' results. She has discovered what is missing from most marketing content and how to correct it.

More Resources from MIYPmarketing.com

Questions about social media?
Go to Word of MOUSE Blog
at WordOfMouseBlog.com
&
Listen to Word of MOUSE Podcast.
New episodes 2nd & 4th Tuesday each month.
Available on iTunes

Want help with your top business challenges?
Listen to some real-world examples from interviews with fellow business owners, who also share their best, and worst, marketing efforts, their biggest business regret and their best business tip on *The Small Businesses Solving BIG Problems Show w/Viver Israel* New episodes on the 1st & 3rd Tuesday each month.
Available on iTunes

Know someone who is 80+ years old?
Help them share their wisdom and insights with the world—
Go to Treasured Wisdom Archive
at MIYPmarketing.com/Treasured-Wisdom

COMING SOON

Website CPR Solution
Breathe life into non-performing Websites & Social Media by completing this FREE online checklist. Website CPR Solution pinpoints marketing problems in Websites as well as social media marketing usage, then generates real-world solutions you can put into action. *Available December 2013*

Home Study Course
Word of MOUSE – Today's "Word of Mouth" Marketing:
How to Use Social Media in Small Business
for Take-it-to-the BANK Results
Available 1st Quarter 2014

www.ingramcontent.com/pod-product-compliance
Lightning Source LLC
Chambersburg PA
CBHW051718170526
45167CB00002B/703